How They See Us

Atlas & Co.
New York

How They See Us
Meditations on
America

Edited by
James Atlas

Interior design by Yoshiki Waterhouse
Typesetting by Sara E. Stemen

Atlas & Co. *Publishers*
15 West 26th Street, 2nd floor
New York, NY 10010
www.atlasandco.com

Distributed to the trade by W. W. Norton & Company

Printed in the United States

Atlas & Company books may be purchased for
educational, business, or sales promotional use.
For information, please write to info@atlasandco.com.

Library of Congress Cataloging-in-Publication Data is available upon
request

ISBN: 978-1-934633-10-6

14   13   12   11   10   1   2   3   4   5   6

Contents

Introduction

James Atlas

The mirror said:
How miserable I am,
No one of those looking at me
Wants to see "me"
—Mourid Barghouti

On the night of September 11, 2001, I leaned out a window of my apartment building on the Upper West Side of Manhattan. The street was deserted; the sky had a strange yellowish tint, even three miles from Ground Zero. An acrid odor hung in the air—the odor of three thousand incinerated bodies. I had read in Holocaust memoirs about the smell of burning flesh that greeted prisoners arriving in the camps, the black smoke rising from the crematoriums. I'd never been able to imagine that smell until now.

The attack on the World Trade Center was unprecedented in so many ways. Never before had commercial airlines been used as missiles; never before had people leapt to their deaths from the top of a hundred-story building; never before had last words been transmitted via cell phone from hijacked planes. And the strangeness of the event wasn't only in the details, which would soon enough become iconographic: Not since the war of 1812 had the United States been attacked within its own borders. (The assault on Pearl Harbor occurred three thousand miles from what was then our western shore.) Until that day now known to the entire world by the numerical shorthand 9/11, we were innocent of history in its most violent form—invasion by air or land or sea.

A child of the 60s, I had witnessed and participated in marches, sit-ins, even riots where the splinter of glass and the hiss of tear-gas canisters mimed the sensory effects of combat (as I knew it from the movies); but my generation, with the exception of those who served in Vietnam, had been largely spared the devastation of war—at least on our own turf. The carnage of the last century, which leveled so many famous cities—Dresden, Stalingrad, Hiroshima, Berlin, whole neighborhoods of London— was as remote from our experience as the sack of Rome. And so it remains. Seven years after the collapse of the Twin Towers, Ground Zero is the epicenter of a battle over commercial real estate. It's hard to remember that people died there.

Forced to respond, we have taken the battle elsewhere. Three days after the attacks, George Bush stood atop the smoldering rubble and vowed that "the people who knocked down these buildings will hear all of us soon." And so they did—along with millions who had knocked down nothing. In a powerful anaphora, the Iraqi-Canadian writer Leilah Nadir describes life in her homeland after the invasion of 2003:

America is a pair of heavy black boots dangling out of a low-flying army helicopter, a machine gun cocked down at me, as I huddle in my night-gown in my cot on the roof of my Baghdad house. America is three thousand cruise missiles landing on my city. America is a tank tread on the fragile remains of the ancient city of Babylon. America is my front door kicked in. America is a curfew that makes it impossible for my great-uncle to get to a hospital at night; he dies of a heart attack at home. America is my teenage daughter, a virtual prisoner in our home year after year, unable to go to school. America is a car bomb exploding in front of my father as he stops in Baghdad traffic, leaving blood and flesh dripping from his arm. America is my crippled brother, a crutch where his left leg used to be. America is white phosphorus, a chemical weapon.

One of the most amazing feats of the Bush adminis-tration was the sheer speed with which it transformed the United States from a victim to an aggressor. The litany of unprovoked acts committed in the name of self-defense is so familiar by now that it can be listed with the same economy as "9/11"—shock and awe, insurgency (which contains within it another mysterious military term, the "surge"), Abu Ghraib, Guantánamo. . . . In effect, the war on terror has itself become a war of terror.

This is not a Bush-bashing book—though the legacy of his calamitous administration will not be easy to undo.

It's not a book about politics or policy, though inevitably they figure in the discussion. It's a book about the deep bond that "foreign" writers—that is to say, writers who aren't American—form with the most powerful nation on earth. "We are not looking for a consensus from the left," we wrote prospective contributors: "We are looking for new vantages, essays written in a strong personal voice. This is going to be an assemblage of writers, not of foreign policy experts."

It was exciting to read their dispatches from around the world as they showed up on my computer screen. (When was the last time an editor received a manuscript in a manila envelope?) Most of the writers we invited are novelists—one significant exception is Ricardo Alarcón, President of Cuba's National Assembly—and their responses, composed with art and passion, are intensely personal. They see us through our literature as much as through our history. The Moroccan writer Abdelkader Benali invokes Ishmael, Portnoy, and Huck Finn, figures as real to him as the World Trade Center (whose destruction he claims to have prophesied while gazing down at the city from its top floor: "What, I wondered, if a little plane flew through this keyhole into the past, present and future. . . . ") Fernando Báez, the director of Venezuela's National Library, reports that as a child he read everything he could get his hands on by Hemingway, Fitzgerald, Raymond Chandler, and Jack Kerouac. "When I began to write, at the age of twelve or thirteen, I was enthralled by Edgar Allan Poe. At my father's behest I memorized the poem 'The Raven' and repeated its verses over and over again."

But their vision of America isn't just drawn from books. I was struck by how obsessed these writers are by popular culture. As children, they form a picture of the American Way of Life from its most shopworn emblems: cowboys and Indians, JFK and Elvis Presley, Rambo and the Terminator, Michael Jordan and Marilyn Monroe (whose habit of not wearing panties becomes for the Mexican writer Carmen Boullosa an obsessive motif). Over time—most of the writers collected here have spent months, even years in the United States, and some live here now—a more nuanced image emerges; more nuanced and more negative. Idealization ends, as it always does, in disillusion.

Coursing through many of these essays is a bitterness that only the betrayed can really know. In almost every instance, it's the war in Iraq that precipitates the crisis of faith. Until our unprovoked invasion in the spring of 2003, we had the advantage in our struggle against Al-Qaeda of a rare global solidarity. People all over the world were stunned by the sight of the Twin Towers crumbling to dust before their eyes. A few leftwing intellectuals saw the attacks as blowback: "To listen to some Americans talk," argues the Marxist critic Terry Eagleton, "one would think that world-history held no tragedy as stark as that of the destruction of the World Trade Center; whereas the truth is that exactly three decades earlier, the United States violently overthrew the democratically elected government of Chile and installed in its place an odious dictator who with US connivance went on to murder far more innocents than ever died in the horror of 9/11." This is, however, a minority view.

One of the spectacles of so much human suffering—the trapped office workers clustering at the windows, the bereft relatives handing out photographs of their missing loved ones—made us a sympathetic ally. At last, the United States was experiencing the trauma of war it had managed to evade for so long, in part because of our overwhelming military power, in part, perhaps, through the sheer luck of geography; thousands of miles from our nearest enemy, we were hard to reach. But the downside of globalization is that it makes everyone a potential target. Isolationism is no longer a viable foreign policy.

Even now, as the war drags on, as civilian and military casualties increase with no end in sight, there is a willingness to cut us some slack. As Fernando Báez puts it: "The United States has been hijacked by a political class with a militarist vocation that long since surrendered, quite unconditionally, to the corporate interests that destroy the environment and manipulate the politics of entire continents, having given in to the commercialization of freedom rather than the freedom of commerce." It's not us, it's our government. Americans are, by and large, still good. We are "friendly," "generous," "open"—to list a few of the adjectives that define us, according to the mostly genial contributors to *How They See Us*. They like visiting our cities; they like consuming the material goods we produce in such astonishing volume; they like our foolish optimism. What they don't like is what we have become.

Given this general decency, why have we been silent about the illegitimate war waged in our name? Among many great mysteries of war in Iraq is the role of intellectuals and the press. Why is there so little protest? Werner Sonne recounts the following exchange between Claus, "who works for a big US pharmaceutical company," and Helmut, "who is a heart surgeon and has lived in California for two years," at a dinner party in Berlin:

> Helmut is upset. About the intellectuals in the US and the media, especially. They are a complete failure, he keeps complaining. The Iraq war, Abu Ghraib, Guantánamo, the constant violations of human rights by US soldiers, by the CIA, how could they tolerate this, how is it possible that they did not protest more, how could they ignore this, tell me, how?

Why didn't American intellectuals object to the war? Why did so many of those liberal and progressive voices who could always be depended on to call our government to account at the first sign of bullying conduct abroad give the neoconservatives a pass? Many were hawkish themselves. They got caught up in the excitement: here was a war, waged on behalf of democracy, that even intellectuals on the left could endorse. (I employ the masculine gender deliberately: support of the war among liberals was largely a guy thing.)

Yet for all our political transgressions, the writers collected here continue to admire us—still want, in a sense, to *be* us. One of the most poignant notes in these essays is the longing not to be seen as the Other. In an impassioned cry of protest, the South African novelist Imraan Coovadia questions—good-naturedly—the whole enterprise:

> The premise of this anthology—*How They See Us*—makes me one of a "them" looking as if through a window at an all of "you." But, like most writers, I have never wanted to be part of a "them"; writing privileges individual judgment and resistance to collective understandings, especially those which we're supposed to have by birth or geography.
>
> People ask, how do you feel as a Muslim? How do you feel as an African? As a South African? Well, writers, just because we create characters, know that viewpoints are plural and contradictory and that one person, not to say one large subset of humanity, can harbor more than one feeling and that these very feelings split and mutate and won't stay still for inspection. And anyway, our feelings aren't necessarily responsible. Like Shylock's daughter Jessica, in *The Merchant of Venice*, we can be attracted by what we see through the window. We can want to join the party on the other side, and sell our mother's ring for a monkey.

Even Terry Eagleton, one of America's harshest critics, praises our "sense of civic fellowship and social responsibility." We are "ruthlessly goal-oriented and noisily self-assertive." Our politicians speak in "a solemn, sententious, mid-Victorian, hideously earnest public rhetoric." We're afflicted with "hubris and hyperbole." But we are also energetic; we have "a bright-eyed 'can-do' attitude." (I was surprised to learn that Eagleton's wife and "two of [his] children" are American.)

A recurrent theme in these essays is the ubiquity of America. We have made the emblems of our culture into universal icons. There is virtually no place in the world where a Big Mac is unobtainable, or a cash advance from Visa. Our presence is inescapable—and oppressive even to ourselves. I often feel a twinge of shame when I travel: you shouldn't be able to speak English in Oslo and Istanbul and just assume you'll be understood. In our national solipsism we have erased all distinctions between people who don't happen to be American: "A Palestinian, an Arab or a Moslem is never shown as a human being, a lover, painter, engineer, neighbor, uncle, a man or a woman with a sense of humor, who would sometimes tell a small lie or cheat in a school exam or even cheat on his spouse," notes the Palestinian writer Mourid Barghouti. We see them as foreigners; toting up casualties of indiscriminate bombing campaigns, we identify the victims as "Iraqi civilians." What Barghouti refers to us as the "*us-them* division of humanity"—*us* being *U.S.*—is more than a tourist convenience: it's a danger to the world. Binary thinking is the enabler of war.

If we have squandered our capital as a Great Empire, we can still live—at least for awhile—on credit. For Da Chen, who came to this country at the age of twenty-three with "a bamboo flute, $30 in my pockets, and the intensity of hope that only an immigrant can know," the

United States is what it has been to wave after wave of immigrants—the land of infinite opportunity. He writes from the vantage of an American citizen—no longer a visitor, but an American writer who lives in the Hudson Valley and whose daughter attends "a very expensive prep school in the Boston area." She shops at Abercrombie & Fitch and takes ballet classes after school. "In my past," Chen writes with ill-concealed anger of his youth in Communist China, "my only after-school activity was carrying an empty bamboo basket around our village's dirt paths scooping up dog poop and cow manure to fertilize our vegetable plots." America has delivered on its promise.

In the end, perhaps, *How They See Us* is about how they would like to see us. It's the America of their dreams—which doesn't make it any less real.

How They See Us

The Rift

Luís Fernando Veríssimo

Translated by Janet Min Lee

One day in July of 1994, I was on an airplane between Dallas, Texas, and San Jose, California. The woman sitting next to me told me that her daughter lived in Kansas. She asked me if that was Kansas down there. It wasn't. Even if she could distinguish her daughter from the landscape, she wouldn't be able to see her. Then she asked me if I knew why the cultivated fields, we viewed from above, were round. Could it have something to do with extraterrestrials? I answered that the shape of the fields had to do with irrigation. Proud of my knowledge of geography and agricultural techniques, I waited for a third question and another opportunity to impress her. But her next question stumped me. She had seen me board the plane with a group of people and asked who we were and what we were doing there. Even if I explained that we were Brazilian journalists en route to California to cover the World Cup, I wouldn't be able to explain why a country with so many problems such as ours could send so many people to cover an event she didn't even know was happening in her own country. I changed the subject.

Before leaving Brazil I'd written some short stories about what we could expect to see in the United States. I wrote, for example, that their "breakfast" explained the Americans. That the Americans were how they were because, on awakening, they didn't simply break their fast. They destroyed it. All American conquests were due to the fact that its civilization was the first in history to eat eggs, bacon, and pancakes with syrup in the morning. The English ate fried fish, and that's why they had lost their American empire. The Native Americans ate chunks of buffalo, the Mexicans their meager tortillas with hot sauce. None of them could stop the power of whole milk. Rifles helped, but the true conquerors of the American West were big breakfasts. The motto of the country, I wrote, could very well be "calorie is destiny." But our arrival in California would coincide with a much more serious lesson about American exceptionalism. If few people, such as my plane companion, knew that a tournament of a foreign sport called "soccer" was to start within a few days, then the fact became even more insignificant in the light of the day's big news: the spectacular pursuit of O. J. Simpson, football and Hollywood star, as prime suspect in the murder of his ex-wife and her lover. When we disembarked in San Jose, televisions showed Simpson speeding away in his Ford Bronco, chased by the police and applauded by blacks wherever he passed. Who'd be interested in the World Cup with a movie like that unraveling in real time?

When you see California from the air, you understand why the political history of the state has to do, in one way or another, with the struggle for water. California is a product of American entrepreneurial might and banditry. The land was taken from the Mexicans and colonized by adventurers. But it is, above all, a product of irrigation. The region we were approaching—San Jose, Santa Clara, and Los Gatos are all part of the same area—is at the base of a peninsula whose tip is San Francisco. These are suburbs, and many who live there work in San Francisco, but the region developed primarily with the emergence of the electronic market (especially computer technology)—and the contrast between the cities' well-kept lawns and tree-lined streets with the charcoal mountains surrounding them gives one a sense of the importance of well-planned water distribution in their growth. At first sight, San Jose seems to embody what Henry Miller meant when he called the United States the "air-conditioned nightmare," just before he fled to Europe. But the sunny charms of the state overcome California's apparent soullessness and after all, even Henry Miller spent his last days on the Pacific coast, having surrendered to its amenities. It's where all of us should go to die.

But we were there to cover the World Cup. Most of the crew were busy installing the equipment and getting to know the neighborhood and didn't notice the pursuit and eventual arrest of "O. J."—certainly the most famous person to be charged with murder since Jack the Ripper, who was rumored to be a member of the Royal Family. Simpson was a hero to many in the black community, but had not necessarily conquered racial resentment. He married a blonde and circulated in the world of white Hollywood celebrities with ease. Everything, including his flight from the police, indicated that Simpson was guilty, but what mattered was that he was a black man making the white man's police run after him. Once Simpson was caught and jailed, the polls diverged: the majority of the white population thought that Simpson was guilty, while most blacks did not. Opinions were divided along an age-old rift that had little to do with evidence or argument. It's a rift that remains despite the numerous black victories in American racial relations, culminating in the election of Barack Obama. The American black experience is the very opposite of what Brazilian blacks know. African Americans were never duped by a false sense of equality and never doubted that they lived in a racist society.

O. J. Simpson was exonerated, but few people believe that he was innocent. Perhaps he killed his ex-wife and her friend certain that his celebrity would, in some way, protect him and clear him of suspicion. In the United States, celebrity in itself has become a value with its own moral universe, defined by the market. Nothing is as profitable as celebrity in the United States, regardless of whether it's due to the discovery of a new vaccine or the castration of one's unfaithful ex-husband. There's a law against people selling the stories of their crimes in books (*How I Dismembered Mommy*) or news stories, but nothing stops those who were involved in a crime from making money off their notoriety. The cast of the Simpson Trial became celebrities, however briefly. Even the district attorney suggested an actress to play her when the movie of the trial came out. And Simpson, the man who, as athlete and actor, had fulfilled the dream of many so effortlessly that we could imagine his being safe from any consequences, must have felt a little like F. Scott Fitzgerald's Gatsby, when he realized that the American promise of a free country where the best dreams of a man could be fulfilled, without obstacles or class prejudices, was nothing but a trap. Celebrity guaranteed Simpson a first-rate defense team and his acquittal, but celebrity did not suspend him above good and evil. And although he believed he had crossed the rift of race forever, his celebrity did not stop the trial from turning into a case of blacks against whites. Same as it ever was.

The United States spent a good part of its history under the illusion that its citizens were the offspring of the European Enlightenment—a product not of crass mercantilism or ugly imperialism, but of Europe's best intentions. Ever since the United States became a nation, there has existed this notion of America as a social experiment, the embodiment of democratic ideals that the old and decadent world could not live up to. The U.S. Constitution was the first explicit contract to ensure a society of equals in the history of the world, and its signers—many of them readers of Locke, Montesquieu, etc.—knew they were inaugurating a republic with novel aspirations. The myths that have shaped American self-esteem ever since—the land of opportunity, the great melting pot, the land of altruism in times of conquest and tolerance in times of victory—originate in the ideal of America as a new start, a regenerated Europe, absolved of the sins of history. The idea survives even today in the illusion that America is a classless society. Thomas Jefferson and the Founding Fathers were rural aristocrats, and the majority of them had slaves. American blacks owe their freedom to the economic war among the agricultural South, the industrializing North, and the pastoral West, although in the country's sentimental history, the end of slavery is attributed one hundred percent to good intentions. That means that from its independence until its judicial battles for civil rights in the 1960s, the Republic lived, with some discomfort but without much damage to its self-esteem, with an oppressed race in its midst, before and after the abolition. It's a defense of Jeffersonian ideals to say that the social equality of African Americans was attained by law—that is, in theory—before it was enacted in the society. It was by desegregation and the use of quotas that white society was forced to absorb African Americans into previously all-white schools. In fact, the whole predicament of dealing with a multiracial society is a New World experiment, of which Europe was ignorant until it started to receive immigrants from its former colonies, like illegitimate children coming to claim their inheritance. Europeans had previously interacted with other races only as subjugators or as the dominant caste. The prophets of the Enlightenment weren't preoccupied with the racial question, because it didn't exist before the 19th century—with the exception of the Jews, and what set them apart was not the color of their skin. The imaginary nation that the Founding Fathers established based on a theory of a moral state lacked European precedents for the master-slave or noble-plebeian relationship, reshaped as the coexistence of "pure" and "impure" races. And the persistence of the racial rift finally unmasked all the other American myths. African Americans won their recognition and their fragile equality in American society in the same way as other suppressed peoples in history— by revolting. After two hundred years of illusion, the United States arrived at an extreme version of the system that symbolized the worst in European class division, the institutionalized distinction in England between landed gentry and the poorest of the poor. With its ghettos and suburbs, abandoned city centers and residential sections simulating pastoral virtues, the United States finds itself with a class-divided society—as Old European as you can get.

On the other hand, of the seventy or so Americans who met in Philadelphia to debate the first democratic constitution in history, the great majority were business-men, landowners, and slave owners, which did not keep them from writing the Bill of Rights, forever defining the equal rights of all American citizens and providing the inspiration for the Universal Declaration of the Rights of Men. Almost 170 years after inalienable rights were secured for Americans, the Supreme Court somewhat belatedly confirmed that the Bill of Rights applied to all races.

The election of Barack Obama highlights the changes that have occurred in race relations in the United States but does not of course mean that the rift is no more. Rather it was a formidable, exultant leap across that rift.

The notion that the "right" to amass property should be conditioned by social concerns was not addressed in the U.S. Constitution. That document was carefully written to protect the landed aristocracy from whatever might challenge its divine rights. Even today, though the rural aristocracy has followed the English landed gentry to irrelevance, no political debate in the United States touches on the question of property. But here too, the assurance of equality in the Bill of Rights persists, like an unfulfilled promise.

At the end of *The Great Gatsby*, Fitzgerald evokes the dream of the new country, caught in its best intentions and contradictions. Fitzgerald describes the West Coast as the "fresh green breast of the new world." Its missing trees "had once pandered in whispers to the last and greatest of all human dreams; for a transitory enchanted moment man must have held his breath in the presence of this continent, compelled into an aesthetic contemplation he neither understood nor desired, face to face for the last time in history with something commensurate to his capacity for wonder." For Fitzgerald, the "orgiastic future" that Gatsby pursued and the promises of the age had evaporated "in that vast obscurity beyond the city, where the dark fields of the republic rolled on under the night." And the enchanted moment would never return.

I don't know if my plane companion ever found out that Brazil won the World Cup in 1994. She apologized for knowing so little about Brazil; but, to redeem herself, she said she really liked Julio Iglesias. I hadn't the courage to tell her that Julio Iglesias isn't Brazilian, he's Spanish. After all, I, too, could be completely wrong about her country.

How I See America as an Iraqi-Canadian
Leilah Nadir

America is a pair of heavy black boots dangling out of a low-flying army helicopter, a machine gun cocked down at me as I huddle in my nightgown in my cot on the roof of my Baghdad house. America is three thousand cruise missiles landing on my city. America is a tank tread on the fragile remains of the ancient city of Babylon. America is my front door kicked in. America is a curfew that makes it impossible for my great-uncle to get to a hospital at night; he dies of a heart attack at home. America is my teenage daughter, a virtual prisoner in our home year after year, unable to go to school. America is a car bomb exploding in front of my father as he stops in Baghdad traffic, leaving blood and flesh dripping from his arm. America is my crippled brother, a crutch where his left leg used to be. America is white phosphorus, a chemical weapon.

America is tiny pieces of metal, mysterious debris from a bomb, collecting in the back garden of my house. America is a group of young soldiers going to church among Iraqi Christians, asking me about the pretty girls they see there. America is waving at me from a tank. America is the concrete blast wall separating me from friends in the next neighborhood. America is a note threatening to kidnap my children. America is a shattered Sumerian vase, a burning library. America is my widowed sister and her fatherless children. America is a hospital without medicine, a house without running water, the deep dark of a power failure. America is loneliness without a telephone as explosions jar the night. America is adolescent soldiers bristling with weapons yelling at me at a checkpoint. America is the bomb that shatters the stained-glass window of my church. America is an overflowing morgue, a cemetery with no room left to bury my great-uncle. America is Abu Ghraib prison reopened as an American prison. America is a soldier killing Iraqi demonstrators who are protesting because the army has turned their elementary school into an army base. America is the Green Zone (forbidden to most Iraqis), once Saddam Hussein's palace and now a paradise of hospitals, electricity, water, swimming pools, cafés, and air-conditioning. America is my great-aunt chopping down the orange trees in her garden to use as firewood. America is her middle-class neighbor digging a well.

America has made me Iraqi. I see America through Iraqi eyes. But it wasn't always so. I grew up in Calgary, Alberta, just a few hours drive from the United States. I am Canadian, born in Canada, raised partly in London, England, by an Iraqi father and a British mother. Until five years ago, America was benign to me. I'd been to Los Angeles, New York, Washington DC, Chicago, Portland, Vermont, New Hampshire, Seattle. I felt practically American myself; I didn't see much distinction between Canadians and Americans.

When New York and Washington DC were attacked on September 11, 2001, I was terrified for my good friends living in both cities, as I couldn't get through on the phone lines. I was relieved when they contacted me a while later saying that they had not been seriously affected. Two years later, I had the same feelings as America was going to war in Iraq; I was afraid for people I knew living in Baghdad. But New York has returned to normality, and five years later, Iraq has not. I could make those anxious phone calls every day.

Until this war, the Iraqi side of my family was silent, muted, their lives impossible to know. The handful of times I'd met my grandparents was in the seventies when they drove from Iraq to England in their Volkswagen beetle for the summer holidays. After that, silence. They died under Saddam Hussein's regime. My father's three sisters now all live in London. Two of them were on vacation from Baghdad when Iraq invaded Kuwait in 1990, and they have never returned. My great-aunt Lina was with them, but she went back early and was trapped in Baghdad when the Gulf War started a few months later. From then on, she looked after my grandparents' house, where my father grew up. In Canada, my Arabic roots were pushing shoots into my being, but never flourishing to the surface of my life.

In 2003, when I finally asked my father why he'd never taught me Arabic or told me stories of Iraq or our family, he merely said, "There was never ever anything good to say about Iraq, so why talk about it?" All my life, he was mysterious and taciturn on the subject, shaking his head at news of the deprivations of the sanctions or the farcical horrors of Saddam Hussein's regime. He often quoted Churchill, saying that democracy was not a perfect system, but it was the best system we had in this imperfect world. He never complained or railed against the circumstances in Iraq that made it impossible for him to see his parents when they were ill or to attend their funerals. He was grateful to be in the "civilized" West. He believed in the United States, felt proud of the Western stance on human rights, the Geneva Convention, the rule of law. As a family, we rarely questioned America's role on the world stage.

The way I saw Iraq was simple. The country was in the grip of an evil dictator who invaded his neighbors, tortured dissidents, oppressed his people with terror, and had dragged my father's once prosperous homeland into violence, poverty, and barbarism. America was the beacon that saved countries from megalomaniac leaders and only went to war in self-defense, did not condone torture, did not invade other countries illegally. In my eyes, America stood on, and for, the moral high ground.

But I never supported a war to depose Saddam. I felt that with the first bomb dropped, America would lose its moral high ground. Under occupation, Iraq has undergone more than five years of unprecedented violence, almost all directed against civilians. At least 650,000 innocent Iraqis are dead, and countless more are permanently injured in a country of twenty-five million. That means nearly one in forty Iraqis have died because of this war. On average, one member of every extended family is dead. It is staggering that Iraq could be worse off than before the invasion, which followed twenty-three years of war and deprivation. But Baghdad is now a city of segregated neighborhoods separated by massive concrete blast walls. Two million civilians have fled as refugees and live precariously in Syria and Jordan without proper status or income, and another two million have been internally displaced. Iraq as it was five years ago, hardly a paradise, has been destroyed, and nothing has yet replaced it. All because of America's invasion.

But even before September 11, 2001, questions were forming in me, doubt creeping in. The Gulf War, and then the draconian UN sanctions that followed, first gave me pause. How could a country be forbidden to import pencils, scientific journals, and medical textbooks? Why were middle-class Iraqis being forced to sell their books for food?

My doubts were confirmed the night the United States insisted on preemptively invading Iraq. The political became personal. Our family was no longer on the sidelines watching the horrors of the nightly news from the comfort of our couch; the USA was preparing to bombard our own family, my father's childhood home. We had been shielded from these same feelings during the Gulf War because Saddam Hussein was the aggressor when he invaded Kuwait. But this time, it was we, of the West, who were the invader. And I knew people who were going to be under those bombs.

I was split in two: blood of both the victim and the perpetrator flowed in my veins. And that mirrored a dichotomy in my worldview. My Iraqi friends' and relatives' voices were growing louder and louder and their stories were at odds with what I heard by means of the Western news media. I heard the narrative in stereo. In one ear, as for all other Westerners, blared the newspapers, radio programs, and television shows. In the other ear, whispers came from afar about how the war was really being fought and ruining my relatives' already desperate lives.

When the war began, I got much of my news via my cousin Karim, an Iraqi Christian, a middle-aged engineer with a wife and two children whom I had never met or even spoken to before. He told me that under Saddam Hussein, America had been banned from Iraq. Iraqis were isolated, with no access to international media, the Internet, or cell phones and no way of knowing anything about the United States. Karim was continually told that America was evil. But he knew that free speech didn't exist in Iraq and that dictators lied, so he did not believe what he was told. But once America patrolled the streets of Baghdad, he had the chance to witness American power firsthand. And through him, I saw the face that America showed the world when it traveled abroad.

I watched through Iraqi eyes as they were invaded by the most powerful army on earth. Karim told me of American bombs shaking his house like an earthquake, of American tanks crushing civilian cars under their treads, of American soldiers shooting innocent people, of my great-aunt guarding our house alone as the war raged around her without the comforts of electricity, running water, or the telephone. I tried to decipher what the U.S. army was doing and what that meant for my family. I hoped with them as they waited desperately, against all reason, for the democracy that all the violence was supposed to bring.

And as I listened to their stories, I struggled to make sense of our narrative, the one that always diminishes the crimes we commit and amplifies the crimes carried out by others. In the chaos of information coming from the television, there was no coherent story. The events after the invasion ended up being nonsensical and abstract for the Western listener, who then went numb and turned off. It's as if they couldn't see the American army occupying the country; they couldn't see that the cause of the violence was the American invasion. And so they can say in complete faith, "We can't leave now, because think of what will happen if we leave?" As if the Americans are the last glue keeping the country from falling apart, instead of the aggressors that broke the country in the first place. A Canadian friend once said to me that when she heard Middle-Eastern news she found herself thinking that the people deserved what was happening to them. It was the only way she could make sense of the news, the way she distanced herself from the horror—to think that there must be a reason it was happening to those other people and not to us. But we have to look deeper—things do make sense; if they don't, it's because we are not looking at the situation in the right way.

Just before the invasion, one of my father's Canadian friends tried to read out some Arabic phrases that the American soldiers had been given to say to Iraqis. My father couldn't understand a word he said. My father tried to imagine an American soldier telling an Iraqi to stop at a checkpoint, the Iraqi not understanding and then the soldier thinking the Iraqi was purposely ignoring him. The results of this misunderstanding are fatal.

As it happened, the first story Karim told me was of a family he knew who were coming home from a visit to their elderly parents on the day that the U.S. army entered Baghdad. Many people didn't know that the Americans were in the city, as Saddam Hussein's regime was still denying it. "Suddenly they saw an American tank up the road," Karim wrote to me, "and without warning, the tank began to shoot at the car with the huge tank machine gun. Instantly the father and their three children were killed. My friend's daughter survived and leapt out of the car, waving at the soldiers to stop." The soldiers started shooting at her. "She ran through the shooting and found a house. It was a miracle she survived. She was taken back to her father's home. Her clothes were soaked in blood. She was like someone who had lost her mind. A few days later, her brothers went to the place where the catastrophe had taken place, but the Americans wouldn't let them near the site. After five days, they were allowed to take the bodies, which the Americans had buried quickly, using only a shovel to dig the shallow graves. When her brothers asked the Americans, "Why did you kill this family?" the answer was simple. "We are sorry, it was an accident."

America changed for my father, too. A successful businessman, he'd visited the United States many times. Then, in November 2003, on a trip to Texas to visit friends, he was taken aside and questioned by the customs officials. Why? Because he was born in Iraq, even though he told them that he left there in 1960 and had never returned. "Do you have allegiance to Iraq?" they asked. He replied, "If by that you mean do I feel connected to the country because I was born there and my parents lived out their lives there, then yes. If you mean to ask whether I am going to return there to fight you, then the answer is no." They let him through, but he was livid and hasn't returned to the USA since. Wasn't Iraq supposed to be a friend of America, rescued by America, on the same side as America? Wasn't that what the politicians were telling us? The question of allegiance implied that Iraqis everywhere were not to be trusted: Iraqis might be the enemy. It implied he was potentially a criminal because of his ancestry.

In the five years of the occupation, my cousin Karim has personally experienced extortion, dangerous run-ins with soldiers, threats from militias, and literally dozens of car bombs exploding terrifyingly close to his house and office. And he survived the three weeks of the actual invasion in 2003 ("the most miserable days of my life" he calls them). When his businesses were threatened, he was forced to close them. Soon his entire family was living under virtual house arrest, rarely venturing beyond the garden wall for fear of death.

Even the Old Testament's long-suffering but faithful Job had his limitations. It took five years for Karim to break, but when, like Job, the threats menaced his physical self, he could withstand them no longer. When the danger of kidnapping literally knocked on his front door in the form of a man he'd been warned to be afraid of, he knew the time had come to flee. This was the last blow to his family, who had survived the crescendo of violence caused by the absence of law and order. This anarchy, the ugly side of the American's cherished freedom, has destroyed all remnants of civil society and ordinary life.

On September 12, 2007, Karim and his wife, teenage son, and daughter, each clutching a single suitcase, got into a taxi and headed toward the Syrian border. They left behind four empty houses they and our extended family owned in Baghdad. One of them was the house my father grew up in, that he inherited when his parents died. Since the Gulf War, my great-aunt Lina had been the house's custodian and guardian. When she died, two years after the 2003 invasion, our cousins took over that role.

My father asked Karim to fill an extra suitcase with any of our family documents or photos he could put his hands on. But there were rumors that Syrian border guards were suspicious of any written documents, so Karim couldn't bring anything. They left behind private possessions collected over six decades: my aunts clothes were left hanging in the closets; family photograph albums made by my grandfather when he was unable to see his family stayed in their drawers; letters written home by my father after he left in 1960 to study in England, and even a family newspaper he wrote when he was a bored schoolboy one long hot summer stayed in their boxes. But on a whim, as he took his last hurried look through our house, Karim grabbed an oil painting.

The painter, Ammu (uncle) Ibrahim as he was known to us, was like a brother to my grandfather and is my father's namesake. Now ninety-five, Ammu Ibrahim lives in northern Lebanon. This painting is of Safita in Syria, the Christian hilltop town covered in olive groves where my grandfather Khalil was born (he moved to Iraq in his twenties), and where my father went on summer holiday as a boy. Khalil's house still stands in Safita, though it, too, was lost to our family, during the Lebanese civil war. As our family fled Iraq forever, the image of Safita, another lost part of our heritage, was the only item they salvaged.

The taxi broke down in the desert and they were stopped and questioned by American soldiers but finally made it into Syria. All this occurred in the week that President Bush was hailing the success of the so-called "surge" and saying that Baghdad was becoming safer. Our cousins have settled temporarily near Damascus. Karim describes the town and its churches as bursting with Iraqi Christians. Christians made up about five percent of the Iraqi population under Saddam Hussein's regime, but they have been fleeing in droves since the invasion.

I can sum up how I feel about America now very simply. I used to blame Saddam Hussein, a hideous dictator and tyrant, for destroying Iraq and making it impossible for me to claim my birthright to one half of my lineage and know the country of my father's origin. Now George W. Bush has achieved what Saddam Hussein never did; he has destroyed Iraq so thoroughly that the ties to our homeland have been irretrievably severed. From the days when my grandparents and great-aunts and -uncles spent the summers with us, I have dreamt of one day visiting Iraq. I imagined seeing the city where my father was born, I saw myself entering the house my father grew up in, and meeting my extended family. We hoped that when Saddam Hussein died, his regime would die with him and Iraq would recover and we could return. But the opposite has occurred. Because of America, Iraq as my father knew it, as my aunts knew it, as my cousins knew it, is gone forever. We have lost Iraq, lost our house, our city, our roots, our heritage. And my cousins have lost their home and their country, their family and their friends.

Meanwhile back in the West, it is the year of an American election. But none of the candidates for president are saying much about the war. In fact, John McCain has been quoted saying that it wouldn't matter to him if it went on for a hundred years. Our only vague hope is Barack Obama, who at least calls it a war that should never have been fought. The media has moved on, the "surge" is being touted as a success, we watch feel-good stories about how the refugees are starting to return to Iraq. But Karim tells me that Baghdad is just as violent, nothing has changed, and he is terrified for his brothers and their families who live near Sadr City. He is depressed watching the Arabic news in Syria, which shows the daily killing of Iraqis that our media doesn't bother with anymore.

I attend dinner parties in Canada, my anger brewing as I listen quietly while men explain the problem with Islam, with terrorism, with the Middle East, why we need to be fighting in Afghanistan and Iraq, why they need our help, the progress we are making, the long battle ahead. I think to myself, "This is the way we discuss the world in North America; it's all abstract and geopolitical." Prices are worth paying, as long as we are not asked to pay them personally. Some people even state that Iraqis should be thankful that the Americans saved them from Saddam. No one ever asks me what I think, even though they know I'm Iraqi, and I wonder why they don't think I would have insight into a land they know nothing of, a people they've never spoken to. They prefer the experts of the newspapers and television news. I could speak up, but I am blocked. I am aware of the chasm that separates what I know and think from what they want to believe. I don't know how to begin, how to explain the scale of the destruction, which is so massive and of which we are really all so blissfully ignorant—and culpable.

Today I received an e-mail from Code Pink, a group of American activists who are passionately dedicated to ending the war in Iraq. The U.S. Congress is about to authorize another 178 billion dollars for the war. I wonder how many people's deaths will be bought with this money. I wonder what the congressmen and -women feel they are buying. And I wonder why Americans have failed to draw any connection among war spending, the price of oil, and the tanking economy. And do they know that this money is borrowed money, this war is running on debt, not taxes, and so it is actually the next generation that will pay the bill? Why aren't they revolting, marching on Washington, demanding that Congress stop pouring money into a war that has only made more people around the world despise America? But there was hardly a whimper of protest on the fifth anniversary of the war. I can only conclude that Americans don't care what is done in their name.

In January last year, I spoke to Karim and asked him how he felt about Saddam Hussein's death, images of which were filling our TV screens. He laughed, saying that Iraqis were starting to feel nostalgic for the good old "regime days" as he called them. Many of them wished Saddam Hussein was back in power because at least under him they had security, jobs, basic life necessities, and even a few comforts. When I told my father what Karim had said, he said, "Well, well, George Bush must be pretty bad if he can lose a popularity contest with Saddam Hussein."

A Stranger among Them

Alberto Fuguet

Now, you hung with me when all the others
Turned away, turned up their nose
We liked the same music, we liked the same bands
We liked the same clothes
—"Bobby Jean," by Bruce Springsteen

1.

Strange, but when it comes to thinking about the USA, the first person that comes to mind is me.

And I'm not even American (eh . . . *North* American, *Estadounidense*). No green card, no residence, no passport; just a J1 sometimes, usually a B1-B2. But as I write this, at a Kenyan Roast–scented Starbucks in Santiago de Chile, the city where I live and was born, the city where I write and set most of my work, I can't seem to be able to answer—to *know*—how we (we? who?) see *you*.

"Them."

Sorry, "Us."

Us?

Who?

How They See Us, that's the title, right?

I mean, you.

Us, them, all, everyone.
I get confused.
I'm really confused.

2.

Note: When I write "us" (or Us if it's in a title or is the beginning of a sentence) I feel as if I'm writing *U.S.* (*yü es*) the abbreviation or nick of USA, which, actually, should be written (or was written) as U.S. of A., or just USA.

Somewhere along the way, the dots disappeared.

Does this happen to everyone?

Just for the record: the U.S. is not the same as us.

Another thing: why do people in the USA call the United States of America "America" ?

Why don't they call it "the States"?

3.

Maybe the whole problem—this image/PR problem that *you* have—is, in the end, or at it's core, linguistic. Americans (OK, you guys win, it's hard to write "United Statesians" and "North Americans," which is not really fair or true) by and large don't speak any other language and a fair amount of the rest of the world is able to speak or understand English. You don't understand us and we understand (or try to understand or want to understand) you.

You, me, them, us. . . .

Ironic: even the title of this collection of essays walks a thin red line.

How They See Us.

Typical self-centered, We-Are-The-World type of lingo.

Not: *How We See Them.*

At least, as a friend commented, it's not titled *Them.*

Them, like the killer, mutant ants from that fifties movie.

Them as in *us*, the *rest*, the *others.*

Maybe too scary.

Another friend: It's a good title, since it's actually about *them*, third-person plural. *How They See Us*, perfect.

Perfect if you are in America. If you are or feel that you are in the center of the world.

But they *are*, says another. Do you think we would do a book about how they see *us*?

A film critic friend adds: they *don't* see us, period.

I think: I don't even want to know how they see us.

4.

It always ends up with the annoying idea that Americans see the rest of the world as *them* (*those* people, *those* Mexicans) and we—the others—see Americans as . . . as *them* as well.

Ellos.

Esos americanos.

Sometimes *them* is a way to situate *them* in another league or universe. They are at the top, the biggest/most powerful country of the world. Other times, most of the time, such as in these harsh times, *them* is a put-down. As in those *putos americanos*. Those fucking ugly. . . .

And yet. . . .

And yet, it's not that simple; it's all so so so complicated.

Puta la huea complicada, puta la huea enredada, puta la huea pajera.

Perhaps George W. Bush's lethal legacy was to be able to untangle a very tangled, intricate, incestuous and codependent, unspoken, hush-hush relationship between you and us. To invent an axis and be able to make the rest of the world take sides.

Our side.

But it's hard, even for the most venal anti-Americanist, to escape the claws of American culture. You always can find a Coke even in the darkest basement full of leaflets and Molotov cocktails.

5.

I'm writing this in English. Trying. I like English, like it a lot. Like books in English, like songs, movies, HBO series. English used to be my language. It was my mother tongue. My first one.

Let me be brief and brief you since I'm going to tell you soon a story about U.S. hatred, anti-imperialism, the works; to tell this story, I need to lay down some context.

This is the context: I was conceived in the USA, born in Chile, came back as an infant, ate Gerber, Wonder Bread, Count Chocula, Chef Boyardee. I watched *The Brady Bunch, The Partridge Family, Mister Rogers.* I grew up in suburbia, California, LA, San Fernando Valley, Encino.

I didn't live in a Latino barrio or ghetto.

All my friends were Jews. We didn't speak Spanish. I didn't. My parents spoke to us in Spanish. Then we went back. They took me back.

To Chile. To Pinochet's Chile. Black-and-White, post–9/11 (the *first* 9/11, the day of Pinochet's coup in 1973) Chile.

I had to learn Spanish, had to turn myself into a Chilean, a Latin American.

I had to learn to hate the USA.

To not be a gringo.

I couldn't. I wouldn't.

I didn't know how.

6.

It's very hard to escape American culture and quite impossible not to surrender to (or at least take a stance on) America's biggest invention: pop culture. A couple of months ago, in a class I taught on twenty-first-century Latin American Literature at UCLA, one of the insights we established was how permeated and, in a way, linked it all is. As a student inquired: is pop culture Latin American or Japanese or French, or just an academic disguise to conceal that all the culture and media is American from its genesis, and, whatever may happen, its DNA is, like it or not, red, white, and blue? *Betty la Fea*, she said, is Colombian; *Ugly Betty* and Salma Hayek are Americans.

I've always ended up feeling excited/exhilarated/ attracted (even repulsed or saturated) by American culture. Wim Wenders said it once, way before Germany reunited: the USA colonized our unconscious.

It sure did mine.

7.

Maybe it's not such a bad idea: to call this essay "Them."

Or, perhaps, "A Stranger among Them."

Because, to be a gringo ("green-go"), to be an American, is always to be somebody else. Depending on the times, sometimes you can be a gringo *de mierda*, gringo *culeado*, gringo *maraco*.

Or just gringo.

Call me gringo.

They called me gringo.

From the start: el gringo. The American.

It could have been worse, a lot worse. Most of my classmates' nicknames were so degrading you couldn't use them in front of their mothers.

But still, to be a gringo. . . .

It's been a long time since I was called a gringo. Since college. Once I published my first book I was called something else, something I don't always like. I'm now referred to as Fuguet.

Hey, Fuguet.

Fuguet dijo esto, piensa esto.

Me carga Fuguet, me encanta Fuguet.

I'd like to be called Alberto.

I hate being called just Fuguet. It's like gringo, just more specific.

8.

Like a rich kid in a public school, to be a gringo, to be an American, is, generally, a good thing.

A cool thing.

You can take advantage of being this creature from the other space. To be an American before the Internet, before information became available, before globalization, had its advantages. Actually, to be in junior and high school in the mid- and late seventies was, in fact, a shield. In a way, the USA was protecting me. Jimmy Carter was my secret superhero, and all the music on the radio, all the shows on TV, all the movies on the screen, were proof that paradise—my paradise, my paradise lost—existed.

Then came Reagan.

9.

By and large my family supported Pinochet. Many people did. They supported or couldn't care less or were afraid or lazy. This happened years ago, but if everybody had a strong hold against him, as the political myth says, he wouldn't have lasted so long.

When I was a school kid, Pinochet was, in my sheltered life, a white noise, a backdrop. End of story. One adjusts quickly: the curfew, those who couldn't come back in, those who suddenly disappeared. But all this was something I learned later. To be truthful, I can't say I suffered what I didn't suffer. During high school, I had high-school problems. Pinochet was in power, but disco ruled. Disco was, in my sheltered adolescent world, the enemy.

Then came college. University. The University of Chile, the public university, the place where students from all places of the social, political, and economic order gathered for a brief time. I entered Journalism; it was part of the Maoist-inclined Humanities Faculty. The Journalism School wasn't on the Humanities Campus; it was left to its own devices, close to downtown Santiago, in an abandoned but renovated torture house that had been used by the DINA (Pinochet's secret police).

This is where I studied; the culture, the language, the clothes were definitely Communist. PC: el Partido Comunista, or, since everybody was young, la *JOTA*, the *JAY*, was the one who decided who, what, and where and how things could and should be carried out. The *JOTA* was the nickname for the *JJ CC—Juventudes Comunistas*, the Communist Youth. They were many and they all held secret identities and met in secret places, though at Journalism School it was no secret. While the whole country was ruled by the strong fist of Pinochet, there, in that school, Communism was king.

I guess these seventeen- to twenty-three-year-old kids who dreamed of Poland and Nicaragua and Cuba didn't really want to establish a Communist regime, but a couple of unwanted Communist babies appeared that had dead-hero names such as Salvador, Victor, or just invented names such as Amaranta, which is a dark shade of Russian red.

What united all these kids, those who were in the JOTA and those who were Jota-Friendly, was a common wish to expel Pinochet. Since this happened in the early eighties, to tumble Pinochet was more than wishful thinking, so the real bond, what linked all the factions, was an unmitigated, unrepentant hatred toward all things American.

From ketchup, music, and movies to foreign policy.

I always understood that a government, or part of it, did not represent a country or stand for it or have to be confused with its people or culture. An administration lasts four or eight years. Maybe more. When Pinochet insisted that the world hated Chile, that they were *contra* Chile, I knew it was not true: they were against him, his policies, his rule.

At the Escuela de Periodismo this was not understood. Reagan was not the problem. *America* was.

Americans were the real problem: *they* were ones that voted for Reagan, *they* saw those movies, ate that food. America, America, the land where liberty is a statue, as the famous Nicanor Parra poem goes. America: Vietnam, Guatemala, Iran, the Philippines, Chile.

Pinochet, it was understood, was one of America's gifts to the world.

This was the end of the Cold War and there I was in this small journalism school in Santiago de Chile.

The war was burning and you had to take sides. I didn't want to.

Then came the invasion of the small Caribbean island of Grenada.

10.

I should have foreseen it. This anti-American spirit. The idea that all that was touched by or related to the USA was tarnished with the original sin. Americans were dumb, fat, obsessed with baseball, cowboys, malls, and giant sodas. Americans were racists, liked to kill each other, and liked to invade. All real culture was European. One had to go see Godard or Fassbinder, not Steven Spielberg or George Lucas—or even Woody Allen, which was considered too American for the *JOTA*'s taste.

I once threw a party at my house. It was during my big Bruce Springsteen phase. "Born in the USA." I understood it was an ironic title. But a friend from those days told me it was not ironic enough. Those jeans, that T-shirt, that flag, that sound. Perhaps Springsteen was criticizing the USA, but he also *was* the USA. (Even Joan Baez is, in the end, so American in her anti-American way.)

When half of my schoolmates left my house in disgust due to the music (even though half of it was British) I learned a real lesson: it wasn't so much a political thing, it was an ethic and aesthetic thing. It was a cultivated, much nurtured rejection.

We were (are) not them, I think the train of thought goes. We didn't have the power but we had the moral strength. They felt superior, empowered, enlightened, in that rejection. Superior and saintly. They were able to renounce those worldly, American temptations.

I couldn't.

The day after the United States invaded Grenada in 1983, I got up and, without actually knowing what had happened, or what or why Grenada was important, went to the Escuela de Periodismo. At lunch, I saw there was a bonfire in the courtyards, along with leaflets, signs, and a great big false American flag made out of a white sheet, written over with black spray paint: *muerte a los americanos.*

Death to all Americans.

I remember our strong, braided Communist leader. Perhaps she wasn't a commandant, just a leftist leader. But she did lead. She was an intense young woman who dressed like a combination of Frida Kahlo, Rigoberta Menchu, and a Bollywood extra. Her eyes boiled anger and resentment, and when her eyes locked with mine I knew I was in trouble.

I knew this was a turning point.

Look, gringo, mira . . . mira lo que han hecho.

Gringos culeados, fucking gringos.

Suddenly a big, anxious mob, high on anti-imperialism, began insulting me.

Me.

I was Reagan, I was the Marines, I was the USA, I had invaded little Grenada.

Gringo culeado, gringo de mierda.

I knew what they wanted me to do, what I had to do.

Was I a real gringo, a CIA agent, or one of them? Was I for the invasion, for Reagan? To listen to Springsteen and have a crush on Diane Keaton and read *Rolling Stone* and Salinger and Bukowski had a price.

Even if all these people were not the enemy, they worked for him.

I had to take a stand.

I had to make them understand that I was pro-American but not that American.

So I did it.

I did what was necessary to calm things down, to show that I was just a stupid kid with bad taste and bad judgment and that I wasn't was a real, hardcore American. I was one of them. I could be trusted.

So I took the soiled fake flag and threw it to the fire.

While it burned, I felt the applause, the cheers, the backpats.

Buena, gringo.

Puta el gringo buena onda.

Then I turned around and walked home. I wasn't proud—I was disgusted—with what I had done. And worse, I was still a gringo.

Just a "good" gringo, a gringo that burns false, badly painted, ten-striped American flags.

Us versus *them.*

Them? Us?

At the end it was just *me.*

Me and my American hurt, my American scars, my American collective shame I had to bear because of my past, because of my tastes, because I didn't like the same music, the same bands, the same clothes.

A Double Life
Da Chen

I came to America at the age of twenty-three with a bamboo flute, $30 in my pockets, and the intensity of hope that only an immigrant can know. In 1985, the Chinese government allowed its outgoing students to change our soft currency into only the exact equivalent of $30, no matter what their destination. China was poor then, hungry for the hard coin of foreign currency, and they cared little that their students could starve soon after arrival at their port of call. Let them suffer, so they would taste the bitter flavor of degenerate capitalistic countries.

My flute was made of bamboo grown in south China, where my little village was. It was a sentimental object for me because it was my father who, without much money, bought it for me when I was eight with twenty pennies from a toothless flute maker who grew fine-knuckled bamboo trees in his back garden. Father had taught me a rich repertoire of traditional tunes and ancient melodies. It was his gift to me, and each time I played the flute, the feeling of homesickness would fade away and I would feel embraced by the warmth of our deep south and the love of my family. I was not a Chinese James Galway but I was never too shy to offer my music, whether for a church service—I was attending Union College, a Christian school with a very big and new chapel on their Lincoln, Nebraska, campus—or a community center. I soon became the music person to go to whenever a singer for the church was late or an organist called in sick. But more importantly, the flute was something of my father, who had since passed away, and each time I played his flute, I could feel his presence. The $30 did not last long but that flute is still with me, a vintage now, mellowed with my spittle.

From Lincoln, I was accepted into Columbia University's law school. After graduating, I followed the fad at that time and plunged into corporate finance, joining the investment-banking firm of Rothschild, Inc., as an associate in mergers and acquisitions. The job came about because I had worked the prior summer for the international law firm of Skadden Arps in Beijing, helping their American clients to deal with Chinese joint venture partners. The job paid me $1,000 a week, a princely sum. I was a one-man show, representing the mighty Skadden on a bicycle, delivering exorbitant American-brand legal service. Skadden's lengthy legal documents had, on several occasions, jammed all of the three available fax machines in the Beijing Hotel, Great Wall Hotel, and Jian Guo Hotel.

The Skadden experience led to a friendship with Robert Pirie, a leading lawyer-turned-banker and former Skadden partner, who was the CEO of Rothschild, Inc. Rothschild was a venerable investment-banking firm headquartered at One Rockefeller Plaza, its hallways decorated with austere portraits of the five original Rothschild brothers. Mr. Pirie had a private kitchen built on the twenty-ninth floor, right behind his office, and had the top French chef from Lutèce cooking for him. The firm's clients dined in rooms overlooking Rockefeller Center's skating rink while drinking the famous house wine, Chateau Lafite Rothschild. Deals were discussed and lasting relationships created.

I still remember my first day at work there. I had on my brand-new suit and hand-stitched Church's shoes, which I had bought at the painfully dear price of $150; both purchases were made possible by my signing bonus. It had been recommended to me by the senior vice president above me that it had to be Church's shoes—no more cheap stuff. My ties were all shiny, bought on a Chinatown street corner for a dollar each. I loved shiny things, anything machine-made: when I was growing up as a child in backward China all the clothes we wore were unshiny rough fabric, hand-stitched by my grandmother.

As soon as I stepped off subway train number 7—which I rode in daily from Flushing, Queens, where I rented a tiny apartment—and emerged onto Fifth Avenue, a torrential rain started to pour. Still very much a village man at heart, who had not owned a pair of shoes until the age of nine, I was horrified that the rain would ruin my brand-new shoes. So I took off my shoes and socks, and put them inside the safety of my faux-leather briefcase (Flushing is a good place for buying such commodities), jamming them in with my lunch box, which contained fried rice left over from the dinner I had cooked myself the night before, and walked the several long blocks to my office without shoes. Good thing Mr. Pirie didn't see me that way, or he might have let me go then and there.

Work consisted of corporate mergers and acquisitions between American and Asian corporations seeking to expand or align or swallow or divest one another. It was tedious and quite frustrating. Oftentimes we chased deals that never came to anything. Life was spent, day and night, seven days a week, on the phone or on the road. We pored over voluminous corporate financial statements, trying to sniff out hidden windfalls or follies buried in mountainous footnotes of fine print written in contorted legalese. The pay was quite good, though, and lunch and dinners were always free and plentiful as long as it was either work-related, which it always was, or if you worked later than 7p.m., which I always did, usually leaving around midnight. When M&A work slowed down in the early '90s, I threw myself into bankruptcy and restructuring work, representing fallen angels like Drexel Burnham Lambert's and Macy's bondholders where my legal training was valuable in analyzing complex agreements for bond issuance and loan documents, and dealing with bondholders in lengthy multiparty litigation.

I should have been content. After all, I was just a poor fellow from China; not even from the glamorous part of China but from a soggy village in the deep south—the part of China that my own northern countrymen would spit on. In my childhood, I had tasted the gnawing bitterness of starvation during Mao's lean years. Now I could order from the best Midtown restaurants just by telling my secretary, Spencer, what I desired. He would order it and bill it to the current client for whom I was toiling. What more could have I asked for? And yet, something seemed amiss. There was a certain emptiness and mindlessness to what I was doing. What was missing, I knew not; what was needed to fill that hole, I could not tell.

I was almost thirty now, entering my *er li zhi nian*— years of coming to be. Time to marry and have children. Only problem: I did not know how to call up a girl and ask her out on a date. It was just not done that way where I was raised. My coastal village in Fujian Province clung tightly to old traditions. No boy should be seen holding a girl's hand, and no marriage could occur without the negotiations of a matchmaker. If you stared at a girl for too long, her father or brothers would go after you, as if you were a thief who had just stolen her virginity. During my law-school years, I dated only vicariously, through the hard work of my roommate. A chemistry graduate student from India, he was doing his blonde Barnard coed every afternoon just a thin wall away from me. Their noise informed me they were having a good time. At the beginning, I was rather annoyed because it distracted me greatly from my studies. Then, slowly, I began to like it. When they eventually broke up, I was the one who wept. But this lack of dating didn't hurt me a bit. I was quite assured of my belief that keeping myself pure for "the chosen one" would hold me in good stead, in keeping with my village virtue, and that belief was finally rewarded when I went on a blind date. It came about during my first year of working for Rothschild.

A dear matriarchal friend, an old-fashioned lady from Shanghai, took me under her wing after having heard my flute music at a church service. She said that it was time I got married. I said, to whom? She said that she knew a friend who had a friend who had a musical daughter of marriageable age going to some California medical school. So we met, and I fell in love. You might think my instant love had come from my lack of contact with the opposite sex. But it wasn't random. I just got lucky. The first woman was the right woman.

Sunny was a vivacious young woman. It was a good name for her: she was a burst of sunshine. She was a special breed known as ABC—American-born Chinese. We proposed to each other on the phone a month after we met, got married a year later, and settled in the suburbs, where she had been raised and where her family still lives. A new generation of Chens came along shortly afterward—Victoria first and then Michael.

Michael, who just turned ten, is picked up every morning right in front of our house by a shiny yellow school bus, and dropped off punctually at our door every afternoon. He has lunch at school and breakfast, too, if he gets there early enough. The teachers are kind and encouraging. No one gets beaten or scolded. At home, he eats Happy Meals, pizza, Chinese takeout, and the occasional home-cooked dinner. After school, we ferry him to an assortment of extracurricular activities: tap, jazz, hip-hop, and tumbling classes in Marlboro; ballet in New Paltz; singing near Kingston; and acting and the occasional audition in Manhattan. In my past, my only after-school activity was carrying an empty bamboo basket around our village's dirt paths scooping up dog poop and cow manure to fertilize our vegetable plots.

My daughter Victoria, thirteen, has been taking ballet since she was three and will be attending a very expensive prep school in the Boston area this fall. What a life she has! She shops for herself in the stores of her choosing—Abercrombie & Fitch, Hollister, Forever 21. She does few chores and is much pampered by her grandmother—my mother, who, since my father's passing, has been living with us. She spends all her leisure time watching her favorite television shows, reading late into the night, or listening to her favorite songs by John Mayer, Beyoncé, or Alicia Keys on her iPod. She is confident about her life today, but even more certain about tomorrow. America instills in her a sunny perception of her own future. So different from my own childhood.

When I was nine years old, at the height of the Cultural Revolution, my family was labeled by the Communist leaders as dirty, rotten landlords—*wu lei fenzi*: one of the five bad elements—part of the former ruling class that needed to be reformed in the new China. My grandfather was no sinner, nor the criminal he was labeled by the government. He had worked very hard to own some land. In 1949, the Red Army took our land, burned my grandfather's deeds, beat him up, and put him in jail. By the time I came of age, I had witnessed my grandfather being slapped across the face by our commune's cadre; my father being hanged by both thumbs; and my diminutive mother struck across her cheek by a brutish militiaman. I myself was ordered to leave my elementary school and became the youngest farmer on that communist farm, getting up very early every morning to collect pig manure. On top of that, I was starving most of the time. Not that our family was lazy. The land was poor and typhoons visited us often, sometimes wiping out the entire season's crop and leaving us with little food for months. Our commune would not allow any "capitalistic commerce" to be conducted. There were months when we ate only one meal a day of soupy rice porridge with much water in it but little rice.

Life was even harder for my sisters. Two of my three sisters never graduated from elementary school, not because there was no school but because they, too, were disgraced. So they became full-time farmers at the ages of eleven and twelve. Every day they had to wake up before sunrise to go to the rice fields to cut rice with older farmers and were given the same amount of labor to do as the adults even though their frames were thin and fragile. They had to carry buckets of mud or manure weighing fifty pounds or more to a distant farm, just as the grownups did. Their shoulders were ripped and bloodied, their backs sprained, their feet blistered: their youth aged, their hope dead. But they could cry only in their own beds, for such was their life; otherwise they would not be given their ration of grains and would starve to death. Such was the child slavery of Communism.

I still remember when my eldest sister Xi Xi came of age, and was ready to be matched with a groom. The matchmaker told my mother that no one with a good political background would touch her, even though Xi Xi was a rather attractive girl. The matchmaker recommended that she be matched to a cripple somewhere far away from our town, so the cripple's family would not bear the stigma of our family's disgrace. No girl liked to be told that she could be matched only to a cripple with a rocking limp, to be his second wife, the first having died of dubious causes. He was also a ferocious drunk. So she waited until she was in her late twenties, facing the dim prospect of becoming a spinster. I was young then, but I understood why she cried alone sometimes in her bedroom.

When I was young, my father often told me never to become a writer though he himself was a playwright who specialized in traditional Chinese opera, and my grandfather was a poet noted for his whimsical verses and eccentric arrangements of meter and rhymes; a couplet of his was painted on our ancestral home entrance: *Colors of the mountain will never leave our door; Sounds of the river will linger forever in our ears.* My great-grandfather was a Jinshi, an official of the last dynasty who had been chosen to be the governor of Putian as a result of his academic and literary achievement in a civil servant examination. Father's reason was simple. If you wanted to be a writer in Communist China, you would have to spout Communist rhetoric and stay away from the untouchable truth of the government's corruption and blatant human-rights violations. If you wrote from your heart, speaking the truth that couldn't be spoken, it would be the most dangerous job you could ever have. Your next destination would be a jail cell with a stinking hole in the middle as your toilet.

For me, it was almost an act of defiance to embark upon the journey of writing my own memoir about growing up during the bloody Revolution. At first, fear held me back, kept me from digging deeper, from touching upon shameful events or painful incidents. Writing about oneself is no less jarring than sticking yourself with a needle or a blunt knife. At first, the writing was terrible, full of big words I had picked up in law school such as *notwithstanding, unbeknownst, therefore, nevertheless, wherein,* and *thereby*. Then, slowly, with each page gently critiqued and edited by my wife, the words began to flow, and the tale formed fluidly on the pages. Sunny read every word and gave encouragement as each event revealed details of my past she had not previously known. When we met in America, I was the portrait of a typical yuppie: starched shirts, cuff-links, briefcase, suit, and tie—the necessary costume of a deal man. The process of writing that memoir became not just a way to reclaim my dwindled childhood, it allowed Sunny to gain an insight into me she otherwise would never have had.

After nine months of furious writing at night and on weekends, small paragraphs became chapters, and chapters grew finally into a completed book of more than three hundred pages. I'd never cried harder or laughed more than during those purgative writing days. All the pain was brought out nakedly again, pain that was soon diminished by the joy I felt revisiting in my memories the good people who had aided me in my growing years. There were plenty of them. I had been ostracized by all the children in school and was befriended by four equally isolated rascals in my village. They became my best friends, protecting me from others' fists and verbal abuse, even though they themselves were vulnerable under the harsh hand of our law and authority. Then there was dear Professor Wei, my saintly Baptist English teacher, who took me from the dirty streets and taught me my first words of English. Her tutoring eventually led me to score well enough to enter college in Beijing, and thus start my journey to America and writing.

The manuscript sat under our daughter's crib for four years. I didn't think anyone would want to publish such a story; it was meant to serve merely as family history for our children. One evening while I was browsing at Barnes & Noble in Poughkeepsie, I encountered a group of enthusiastic writers gathered around a table, critiquing one another's work. I was intrigued enough to pay the $20 annual dues and became a member of the Mid-Hudson Writer's Association on the spot. For the first six months, I sat quietly, just listening to others read their fine prose and poetry, too shy to read my own work. Then one day I finally marshaled enough courage to start reading my memoir. After the first chapter, one man asked if it was fiction. I said no, it was the true story of my life. He said that I'd had a pretty shitty early life. I agreed with him. The group urged me to read one more chapter, breaking the association's one-chapter-only policy. After the third night of my reading, one of the members took me aside and told me that my memoir was good enough to be published. He said he was the national sales manager at Simon & Schuster, in the business of selling books, and offered to pass my manuscript along to one of the editors at his house. When I asked him who would want to publish a little story written by a nobody, he took me to the autobiography section. He showed me a copy of *Angela's Ashes* and told me that this book, written by a retired Manhattan high-school teacher, had won the Pulitzer Prize.

I still remember vividly the details of that unforgettable day when my agent called to tell me that Random House had bought my book. It was a hot summer day. The sky was blue and the sun bright; the grass was very green. There were some thin white clouds hugging the horizon. The phone rang, the old upstate line crackled, and my agent joyfully told me the staggering amount offered. I listened with the receiver pasted to my ear but heard little, my heart thumping like a mad drum and my head buzzing like a tossed beehive. She said much but in the end two words repeated themselves in my head, over and over again, like lingering summer thunder: Random House! Random House!

We celebrated by feasting at the best Chinese restaurant we had in the area. Yesterday my manuscript had just been dusty pages and broken memories. Months from now it would be printed and bound and made available for the whole world to read.

When the book was published, half the town showed up at my first book signing at Ariel Books in New Paltz to cheer me on—half of whom were my wife's patients.

Then I embarked on a thirty-city book tour. There were large crowds and much smaller ones, but the people of America were always kind and welcoming. A Buddhist couple in Chicago gave me a long-stemmed rose, a Woodstock ceramicist made me an ink bottle, and a Minnesota man brought his two sons to see me because they had heard me on NPR. A book club in Iowa wrote to tell me that they had a ritual after reading each book: they pretended to invite their favorite character out for lunch. This time it was my mother whom they had unanimously voted to invite.

In China I would have been swept into a dark prison, known by a number and not a name.

The Message

Ricardo Alarcón de Quesada

Translated by Kristina Cordero

I can still remember when we went out with some friends who were about to discover *Viridiana* for the first time. In a small movie theater in New York's West Village, there were a few other couples, people who looked just like us, upper-middle-class professionals, who were also seeing the movie for the first time. And I can still remember how astonished my wife and I were by the surprised reaction of our friends when we told them that we, like millions of other Cubans, had seen not only *Viridiana* but all of Buñuel's films, and that they had been projected in large movie houses all over Cuba.

In New York, we cultivated lasting friendships and came to know people we will always remember for their inexhaustible capacity for love—it was with those friends that we visited museums, galleries, and theaters, walked down streets and through parks, and traversed the city, a place so striking in its beauty and contrasts. We became familiar with its light and its shadows, and through them we discovered the city's most valuable jewels: the people of New York. For some people, New York is a symbol of arrogant opulence. For others, it is a place to be visited as a tourist, or else to indulge one's consumerist delights in stores with lights that never dim. For us, above and beyond all other things, New York is the people who inhabit it, its hardworking, generous, friendly people. It is those people I think of whenever I proclaim, without blushing, that "I love New York," too.

Among these people I include the many I came across in bookstores and diners, in classrooms and parlors, who would berate me with hostile invectives and anti-Cuban prejudice, but were also able to listen and argue and maybe, in the end, understand my viewpoint, even just a bit.

Over the course of many years, we have had similar experiences time and again. In both New York and Havana I have had countless meetings with American politicians, journalists, businessmen, diplomats, intellectuals, and students where the common denominator has always been the cultural rift that divides us. And perhaps the comment I have heard most frequently is "I didn't know."

More than once, leftist American friends and people concerned with improving relations between our two countries have talked to me, as if it were the most natural thing in the world, about the importance of making an effort to "educate" politicians and other people responsible for making important decisions in Cuba. Such statements, which reveal a sad and easily proven truth, cannot help but cause consternation among those of us who are not from the United States.

This concern begins to take on truly distressing proportions when we think about how those people who do not understand a significant number of basic facts about the world around them also happen to possess a military might that is capable of annihilating the planet many times over.

My principal endeavor, for many years now, has been that of trying to "educate" *them*. I am not certain that I have had any success as a teacher in that sense, but at the very least I have been able to enjoy experiences that, on more than one occasion, have also proven quite disconcerting.

I was able, for example, to show a legislator the text of an amendment that bore his name, endorsing the "embargo" against Cuba. I had to do this because the gentleman in question, no doubt a sincere and well-intentioned man, had boasted of having made a very important contribution toward improving relations between the two countries—that is, until he finally had to confess, dumbfounded, that he had not read the full text of his own legislation.

On another astounding occasion, I found myself in the position of having to explain to a very self-sufficient senior senator that it was not Cuba that was imposing an embargo on the United States but vice versa, and that the Helms-Burton and Torricelli laws had been passed in Washington, not Havana. I think I may have been a bit curt when I explained to him that he had voted in support of both laws, though probably without having read them.

There are other information voids with possibly even graver consequences. On several occasions I have spoken with Robert McNamara, the former defense secretary of the United States. I have heard him here, in Havana, talk about what he knew during the days of the Bay of Pigs invasion in 1961 and then during the so-called Cuban Missile Crisis in 1962. I believed in the sincerity of his anguish, as a human being, over the tremendous responsibility that rested upon his shoulders, a responsibility upon which the lives of so many other people hinged. And I believed him when, forty years later, he acknowledged his own ignorance and admitted that he had not known certain basic facts at a time when he had been charged with decisions that would directly affect the lives of others.

For the past ten years, I have been trying to get Americans to take an interest in the case of five Cubans who, without having caused any harm to anyone, are presently behind bars in the United States and, moreover, are being subjected to deplorable prison conditions, including a prohibition on family visits. Collectively they were given four lifetime sentences and seventy-five years in prison for having sought out—peacefully, without weapons, resorting neither to force nor violence—information regarding the plans of a number of anti-Cuban terrorist groups that operate with total impunity on American soil.

When I mention the names of Gerardo Hernández, Ramón Labañino, Antonio Guerrero, Fernando González, and René González, many of the Americans I speak to tell me that they know nothing of this case or of the heroic sacrifice that these five young men have made. The fact that everything has been duly recorded in official documents that are easily accessible is irrelevant.

The fact that parliaments, churches, and humanitarian, legal, and human rights organizations all over the world have called for their liberation is also irrelevant. The principal U.S. media organizations, "informative" as they are, have said nothing about these five martyrs. Many honest, noble people in the United States have confessed to me, quite simply, "I didn't know."

I have worked hard to make people understand that this matter is one of critical importance for the United States, its politics, and its people. A country cannot pretend to wage a "war on terror" around the globe while protecting some of the most despicable terrorists of all within its own borders, and ruthlessly punishing those who oppose their transgressions in the United States.

The abominable acts of September 11, 2001, provoked a most justified indignation in the United States. On that day here in Cuba, along with millions of other Cubans, my wife, my daughter, and I wept in pain and anger.

We also felt pain and anger when we learned that in early May of 2008, in the city of Miami, a public tribute was held in honor of Luis Posada Carriles, self-confessed terrorist and mastermind of unspeakable crimes that he himself acknowledged in his autobiography as well as in front-page interviews published by *the New York Times* on July 12 and 13, 1998. The event was covered extensively in the media. Pain and anger were what we felt when, in that terrorist conclave, speaking directly to the cameras and microphones of Miami's television stations, Mr. Posada announced the new criminal plans he was hatching against the Cuban people.

A great Latin American poet who was awarded the Nobel Prize once described United States foreign policy with two words: arrogance and ignorance.

Over forty years ago, I was sent to New York as the Cuban Ambassador to the United Nations. There, I shared countless unforgettable hours with many brothers who make their home in New York and who are part of a generations-old tradition of emigration that extends back to the days before the triumph of the revolution in 1959. They are the successors of many others like them, who followed the very same path long before the rise of the Cuban nation.

One spring afternoon, toward the end of a party among Cubans, a compatriot of mine, wizened by many years of long workdays in the factories of New York, told me about a secret he had been hiding in his house for some time, an object that he wanted to give to me before he died, now that Cuba was finally free and independent.

In a humble room in the northeast corner of Manhattan, this man began to rummage through a trunk, from which he produced a picture. It was little more than a modest wooden frame with a glass panel protecting a document that, by this time, was over a century old. I read it.

The document contained a message signed by Carlos Manuel de Céspedes, the Father of the Nation, the founder of the Cuban nation, the President of the Republic who rose up in arms and who, in 1868, proclaimed the liberation of all slaves and launched our nation's struggle for independence and social justice.

The words had been written for the benefit of one of the revolutionary clubs of the patriotic Cuban émigrés living in New York. In essence, Céspedes sent his people two cautionary messages: on one hand he warned them that the United States leaders were beholden to an oligarchy that aspired to take over Cuba and that would always try to thwart its efforts for independence, and on the other hand, he also stated that the people of the United States had absolutely nothing to do with those imperial pretensions, that the Americans were a noble and generous people of a friendship and solidarity that the Cubans would do well to cultivate.

Before me I had a letter that reiterated what the Father of the Nation had explained on so many other occasions, something that José Martí would condemn twenty years later, and that history would eventually reveal to be true. But how had it made its way to the man who was now handing it over to me, a century later?

Many years earlier, before World War II, when he was a young man who had recently arrived in the United States, he had found a job with a construction team, almost all of them Cuban, whose work consisted of demolishing old buildings and cleaning up the remaining debris. This was precisely what they were doing one day in a dilapidated building in Long Island when, by accident, they came across the picture and rescued it from a mountain of twisted scrap iron, collapsed walls, and dust.

They decided to hold onto it. Believing that it would be an insult to the memory of Céspedes to turn it over to the Cuban leadership of the day, they kept it under lock and key during the two Batista dictatorships and the corrupt administrations between them. They kept it in their possession even after the triumph of the 1959 revolution, until, finally convinced that the Nation had finally achieved victory, they granted me the great honor of receiving it so that I might, in turn, send it to the museum where it sits today along with many other national treasures.

Long before anyone else did, Céspedes discovered the secret behind official U.S. policy toward Cuba. Though he traveled to many countries, he never visited the United States, and while on one hand his letter warned of the threat it represented, it also called for friendship between the two nations. This message, so lovingly preserved by the Cuban people, is something that will always stay with me.

A Lesson from America

Andreï Makine
Translated by Geoffrey Strachan

There are only two peoples now. Russia is still barbarous, but it is great. . . . The other young nation is America. . . . The future of the world lies there, between these two great worlds. One day they will collide and then we shall see struggles of which the past can give us no idea. . . .
—Sainte-Beuve, *Cahiers de 1847*

When one is an American decision-maker one turns to the President of the United States as to the Supreme President of a world empire. . . .
—Sébastien Fumaroli, *Tempête Sous un Crâne*

Behind the Curtain

A few years after the end of the Second World War, Hitler was dethroned. In the Russian imagination the demonic figure of the Führer was replaced by that of the American, our chief enemy from now on. Two parallel incarnations of the despicable Yankee remain among my earliest childhood memories: he could be fat or thin. The first would be dressed in a tuxedo, bursting at the seams from his monstrous belly, and chewing on a lavish cigar; he was never without a bag from which gold coins or dollar bills spilled forth. American capitalism incarnate. The other one, easily recognizable as Uncle Sam in his top hat, was as lean as a skeleton beneath his tattered tailcoat and had this odd habit of brandishing an atomic bomb, holding it by its tail fins. The fat man would end up hurled to the ground by workers with fists heavy from physical labor. The thin man, the appalling warmonger, was held in check by a rocklike soldier of the Red Army.

Propaganda posters, of course—caricatures pasted all along the Iron Curtain that, in those days, cut the world into two. Happy times! A blessed era of seeing things in black and white: the wall between East and West was plastered on each side with grimacing monsters. A Red, with a knife gripped between enormous teeth; an American imperialist with his bomb. Yes, it was all reassuringly clear-cut.

But was that simplistic perception we had of the United States in those days such a false one? They told us about American racism, and, in truth, the instances of racial discrimination were rife; they were not all invented by the editorial writers of *Pravda*. Poverty, unemployment? Even the most ardent defenders of the American way of life could not deny the reality. The ideologues who kept watch over Russian brains were never at a loss to produce historically accurate evidence that would demonstrate the harm the American empire had done to the world: The extermination of Native American Indians, slavery, Hiroshima, Vietnam, economic dictatorship, the dubious methods of the CIA. . . .

Meanwhile on the other side of the Iron Curtain, in the West, the opinion makers had an equal superabundance of arguments: the horror of the long decades of

Stalinism, the extermination industry of the Gulag and its tens of millions of victims, the lack of the most elementary political freedoms, and the exporting of this totalitarian system to Eastern Europe, to Asia, to Africa.... The polemical exchanges between two great nations along these lines guaranteed an apparent coherence to the postwar world. One could almost have applauded this strategic ping-pong had it not given rise to innumerable "local" wars, insanely excessive rearmament and, above all, a climate in which Russians and Americans were condemned to hating one another across the Iron Curtain, without truly knowing one another. In the days of my youth, one of the books about the United States that was most widely read was titled *The City of the Yellow Devil.* The city in question was New York and the curiously colored devil was simply a metaphor for gold, for the dollar, for the Americans' legendary greed for profit. True or false? To check it out we would have had to cross the Iron Curtain, past lines of watchtowers. The Moon itself, thanks to Yuri Gagarin, seemed more accessible to us than the American continent, where fat capitalists, skinny warmongers, and other diabolical trash were on the prowl.

Faulkner to the Rescue?

At this stage in my account, good form suggests that I should give the lie to this appalling robot-portrait of the American, switch to a lyric mode, and tell you about the American literature that, like an intellectual antidote, enabled the young Russian that I was to correct this unattractive image of the United States. Writers speaking frankly about their attitude to American civilization often perform such a rhetorical about-face: "Faulkner, yes! Bush, no!" I shall avoid this ploy.

First of all, as I have already said, the criticisms made of your country often seem well-founded to me. Also, true national literature holds up the most pitiless mirror to a people with no wish to remain blind to their own shortcomings. The greats of American literature are not subtle image consultants for the White House but formidable observers of the evils suffered now and in the past by their homeland. Finally let us note with regret that neither Faulkner, nor Hemingway, nor Salinger succeeded in averting the horror of that famous photograph: the sky in Vietnam blackened by napalm, a naked child in tears, disfigured by fear, running along a road.... The books by them that did manage to fly over the Iron Curtain alighted in our hands like weary birds, too rare, too precious, too fragile for us to demand of them that they should redress wrongs and remake the world.

I could allude to other oft-repeated instances: American jazz, the cinema, etc.... But why lie? I have never been crazy about jazz, which musical correctness always insisted that we admire. As for the cinema, I used to prefer what fashion instructed us to despise: the action movies that did indeed seem to me very American in the way they tended to portray head-on collisions between Good and Evil, with their unashamed striving for powerful visual effects.

No, what helped me to resist the propaganda images, what made your country alive and human for me was much more humble. A few objects, a few fragments, I might say. Meteorites originating from the unknown and disturbing planet, more remote than the Moon—that America was to us.

Meteorites

Don't laugh! The first of these is a simple tin can, a large container with writing on it in English, such as one sometimes came across in houses in the Soviet Union. A utilitarian object (people put flowers in them, they stored rice or buckwheat in them). A sentimental talisman as well: everyone knew that during the war it was in these containers that the Americans, our allies in those days, used to send us canned meat. This detail might seem ludicrous, but only if you were to forget that the city of Leningrad alone lost more than a million of its inhabitants, wiped out by famine. As time went by, these empty cans revealed a truth to us that resisted the brainwashing: America, that Evil Empire crammed with bombs, could also be our friend! A very disconcerting truth for ideologues on both sides of the curtain. . . .

So disconcerting, by the way, and so rarely referred to in official history, that during my youth it took me a long time to identify this other American meteorite: a photograph discovered among the books belonging to the old lady who had taken the place of my mother. It showed some airmen grouped around a large troop-transport plane, of a type unlike any Soviet military aircraft. The men, too, had a surprising look about them. I could recognize the clothes worn by the Russian pilots well enough, but these others, who were they? Smiling open faces, a uniform that was lighter, more elegant. Where had they come from, these extraterrestrial beings? The old lady let me in on the secret. They were American airmen delivering military aircraft to their Russian ally. These machines had to be flown to the Eastern Front all the way across Alaska, then across the Bering Strait and across the endless wastes of Siberia. This route, a distance of some four thousand miles, was known as the "Alsib." No history textbooks mentioned it. The memory of that air route, which was superhumanly challenging and called for heroism daily, had disappeared beneath the posters with which the propaganda bosses tirelessly plastered the sticky wall that kept our two worlds apart.

My view of your country, as you will have gathered, is quite a subjective one. I belong to that generation of Russians who were affected physically by the carnage of the last war: among the twenty-five million Soviet deaths attributable to the Nazi invasion, every family lost someone. Many of us children knew our parents only for a short period of time, since they died young, ravaged by the fighting, by illness, by war wounds. Yes, my perception is undoubtedly conditioned by that bygone age when the significance of a food container "made in USA" was not the commercial advertising on the label: it meant the survival of a child, a mother, a soldier.

I have many times since then had occasion to board a plane and fly to the United States. But in my memory the Alsib route remains the flight of my dreams because it taught me what they could be like, the men who lived on the other side of the Iron Curtain.

To make sure the Alsib meteorite was not forgotten, I went to visit the site of that aerial route and devoted a book to the pilots who braved those polar regions. It was a project for a writer or an archaeologist: starting from a few fragments, to reconstruct an unknown civilization.

The Myth of America

One of the most Russian of characters in literature, Dostoevsky's Ivan Karamazov, intended to escape to America. His only goal, like that of millions of human beings, whether heroes of novels or real people, was freedom. Almost a century after Ivan Karamazov, the Soviet diplomat Victor Kravchenko would take the same risk, much more dangerous by that time than it had been in Dostoevsky's. The title of this defector's story, *I Chose Freedom*, has become a hallowed expression, a motto, a cliché.

Kravchenko was escaping from the worst and longest-lasting dictatorship known to humanity. Like all the dissidents who risked crossing the Iron Curtain, he knew that this "chosen freedom" could be the death of him. Indeed it was, in a certain manner, for himself and for his family. He did not seek what was generally desired by people setting sail for America over the centuries: social and professional success, wealth, comfort and—why not?—renown. The fame he did achieve was painful, the material comfort quite relative, the success all too fatal. And yet the simple possibility of being able to speak freely, to escape from the dictatorship's crushing gravitational pull, seemed to be enough for him.

As we saw it from behind the Iron Curtain, what America symbolized was this sudden weightlessness—to use a somewhat cosmic metaphor but one that expresses very well the sensation offered by this freedom we dreamed of: to break away from an alienated, enslaved self and take flight to a radically new world, a new self, a self free to express itself, to move around, to choose where to live and where to work, or else not to work at all and to set out "on the road."

In reality the libertarian dream of America combined a great spectrum of aspirations within it. Clearheaded schemes for personal social betterment, serious missions on the part of truth seekers, and even, on occasion, juvenile fantasies of anarchic escapism. But the point of intersection for all these *American dreams* was always the same: freedom.

This underlying basis for the myth of America, for its new world, has led to a messianic faith in democracy for which the United States claims to be the shining champion upon earth. Let us not discuss the legitimacy of this; let us simply recognize how firm the American conviction is that the torch of freedom is in good hands. It is here that the Russian view, my own among others, may be instructive. For the messianic faith of Communism springs from a rather similar conviction: mankind must be set free! Thus on both sides of the Iron Curtain societies have arisen, each claiming a prophetic, exemplary character. A full comparative analysis of these two messianic faiths would call for a voluminous academic thesis. In my brief account all I can note is this: in that long and cruel contest that was the Cold War, Soviet messianism ended up the loser. But does that necessarily mean that the democratic militancy of the United States emerged as the winner?

An Outcast Messiah

That was the question I asked myself several years ago, when I saw the terrifying abyss opened up by September 11. An event gone over again and again by so many intelligent minds who have striven to explain to us the reasons— and the unreason—for hatred of America. Their bafflement is logical: here we have a country that claims to aspire to the noblest of humanist values; one that welcomes onto its soil people from all four corners of the earth and does everything possible to ensure that these new arrivals should integrate quickly, find a job, feel secure; a country that spends immense sums to defend these democratic ideals throughout the world; a prosperous country on the forefront of technical progress, open to every current of intellectual life, tolerant toward all political opinions.

In short, a model democratic country! And yet... there are many parts of the world where they burn its flag, its rulers are hated or ridiculed, its power identified as that of the "great Satan," yes, that "yellow devil" of the caricatures at the time of my childhood all over again. Who are the fanatical barbarians who dare thus to defy the *Pax Americana*, the rule of the greatest democracy in the world?

There is nothing mysterious about this paradox. The "barbarians" who made their odious terror attacks in

2001 were sufficiently Americanized to pass unnoticed. For them, America was not an unknown and enigmatic land rejected through ignorance. They rejected it because they knew it only too well. And the intensity of their hatred can be gauged by the resolution with which these terrorists went to their deaths. A psychologist with time to ponder might conclude that the very thing these young men, apparently well integrated into Western society, were seeking to destroy was this American essence in themselves. To kill it by killing themselves. And this hypothetical psychologist might possibly be right.

Blowing in the Wind

As one tries to understand the intensity of this hatred, it becomes clear just how hard it is to say what America is. This country is forever under attack for being what it is not; people assail ideological bogeys that Americans would not recognize as their own. Like all great civilizations, America is a mass of contradictions, has many faces, is resistant to all dogmatic assertions. When it is vilified, one may picture it as a monstrous bogey, a scarecrow buffeted by violent bursts of wind and one whose shape and grimaces are constantly changing. Let us take a look at this dance in the wind.

The United States is a formidable economic power, but it is also an overheated engine, shaken by a series of terrible crises. This country possesses armed forces equipped with marvels of technology, but these troops are disabled when confronted by warriors from another era brandishing antediluvian blunderbusses (in Somalia and Iraq . . .). It proclaims respect for human rights and treats human dignity as something sacred but tolerates scenes of abominable torture by American military personnel. The great humanistic credos professed by the rulers of America do not exclude the use of the famous "waterboarding" technique, recognized by the CIA, the horrible practice to which George W. Bush has given the green light. And the celebration of freedom that we like so much about America exists side by side with the covert intellectual slavery of political correctness.

More than once I have found myself perplexed by the paradoxical nature of America. And often, moreover, in looking beyond the bogeys raised by anti-Americanism, I have discovered a completely different reality. "America," they lament in Paris, "is totally unreceptive to European culture." The opposite has always been demonstrated to me by the record over long years of my American publishers, Jeannette and Dick Seaver. "The Americans have little interest in the history of our country," the French intellectuals complain. Yet one of the best-informed experts on contemporary French history is American. DeGaulle and Pétain, Flaubert and Camus, Rothschild and Michelin have all been brought vividly to life in a series of prodigiously well-documented books by Herbert Lottman.

Despite an avalanche of books about the United States flowing into France, the ambiguity remains. We still have to choose between the old clichés of the Cold War: the "great Satan" for some, the shining champion of democracy for others.

To my American friends, astonished by the schizophrenia of such dual perceptions, I recommend a re-

reading of Dostoevsky's *Notes from the Underground*. Its hero advances this hypothesis: tomorrow humanity may well contrive to create a paradise on earth, a peaceful and tolerant society, respectful and prosperous (not so very distant, let us add, from the global regime dreamed of by the shining Yankee champion . . .). And yet even in this perfect world, Dostoevsky imagines, there will always be an implacable killjoy to launch a great kick against this universal harmony. "Simply to show you I'm free!" will be how he explains this gesture.

Beyond all political, religious, or cultural considerations, this parable of the great kick directed against the paradise on earth enables one to understand many things in the psychology of those who do not love America—yes, populations who, instead of tossing roses at the U.S. Army tanks, dig out their old blunderbusses and go off into the hills to fight the GIs.

Believe me, dear American friends, there is no malicious pleasure underlying my words. Long ago, as a young Soviet soldier who believed he was bringing paradise to the Afghans, I was amazed, like you, that our tanks were not strewn with roses as we drove through the ruined villages.

But above all, I believe Dostoevsky was right. For if you want to seek beyond slogans and stereotypes, you have to go back to the human soul: then we can begin to understand the apparently illogical, unreasonable, and violent actions of those who refuse the benefits of our messianic wisdom.

A Forgotten Photograph

My perception of America is extremely fragmentary, derived principally from some trips there, some books read. As for present-day America, how can one judge it? So submerged is it, at one moment beneath journalistic verbiage and at the next beneath learned commentaries dissecting the country for all the world like a mammoth dug out of the permafrost. Yes, America, a mosaic of fragments.

Yet one of the fragments I carry within me faithfully mirrors the whole scope of the panel *America*, in all its richness, with all its contrasts. I am speaking again of that old photograph I saw in my childhood: a great Douglas aircraft, the wings all covered in ice, a group of airmen, their clothes dusted with snow. I have a clear recollection of the American pilots' smiling faces. . . .

These were not men who had come to give the Russians lessons in democracy. These Americans were not there to change the political character of the USSR, nor to overthrow the dictatorship that prevailed there, one beside which a Saddam Hussein would pass for Snow White. They had come to help a people in their fight against the Nazi horror. Without making any show of their superiority, they gave us all they had: their courage, their expertise as pilots, their determination, and, on occasion, amid the arctic wastes, their lives.

They were in no way tempted to act like condescending benefactors, like umpires monitoring the ascent toward democracy. For the Russians, their mere fraternal presence became the best lesson in humanity.

The Soviet airmen who rubbed shoulders with them learned a great deal: "so, those appalling American imperialists could also be these guys with open smiles and unfailing courage." It was possible to live like them without flinching at every word you spoke in case it led to your spending years in the Gulag. It was possible to have a good laugh together, exchange jokes, listen to the stories told by these enemies of yesterday, whose lives suddenly seemed so close, so humanly close.

The squadron of Douglas and Aircobra aircraft would take off from Alaska, heading toward Siberia, and from their cockpits the Russian pilots would see a cluster of men in the middle of an expanse of snow waving their arms in farewell. No propaganda could erase that vision of America. That lesson from America.

When it falls to me to comment on the part the United States has to play in the vast concert of nations, I like to call that old photograph to mind. For this, I believe, is how, amid all the discordant sounds, a piano tuner ensures that the true note he is seeking rings out loud and clear.

It Can Only Get Better
Werner Sonne

A walk down Kurfürstendamm, the main artery of the old West Berlin, almost makes an American feel at home. Within a mile or so you can find four Starbucks, the unavoidable McDonald's, Burger King, Kentucky Fried Chicken and Pizza Hut, one huge Levi's outlet, and one even bigger Niketown shop.

Same thing at Potsdamer Platz, the heart of Berlin, with its many movie theaters. Two thirds of all movies shown here—as in the rest of Germany—originate in the United States. When February rolls around, it's time for Berlinale, which has evolved into one of the world's leading film festivals, and the red carpet is crowded with American star power, cheered enthusiastically by thousands of German fans.

American lifestyle and American pop culture are here to stay. Yet the distance between the USA and Germany has never been greater in the past half century. And the rift not only divides the two countries; it splits the Germans, too.

Let's ask Claus, who works for a big American pharmaceutical company, and Helmut, a heart surgeon who lived in California for two years, facing each other at a dinner table in Berlin recently.

Helmut is upset. About the intellectuals in the USA and the media, especially. They are a complete failure, he complains. The Iraq war, Abu Ghraib, Guantánamo, the constant violations of human rights by U.S. soldiers, by the CIA, how could they tolerate this, how is it possible that they did not protest more, how could they ignore this, tell me, how?

Claus, on the other hand, argues that we still share the same values with Americans. And after all, we still owe them. Shouldn't we be a bit more thankful?

But Helmut is not ready to make any concessions. He has had it with these Americans. The more he talks about it, the more he gets agitated. It is clear what drives him, it's a love lost, his admiration for the USA, for the American dream, for the land of the free. He is shattered, a man deeply disappointed and frustrated.

Helmut is not alone in his frustration. He echoes a sentiment shared by millions of Germans who grew up in war-ravaged, divided Germany believing America was the role model: a working democracy with a deep love of freedom that stood up against the Communist threat and kept West Berlin a free island with the airlift.

A whole generation of Germans, the baby boomers of the late forties, remembers the Americans as a generous people, feeding a starving nation with their CARE packages.

John F. Kennedy was their hero, the man who said, "Ich bin ein Berliner"—"I'm a Berliner"—after the Wall was built.

Yes, there was friction during the Vietnam War, and Ronald Reagan was not really trusted, but overall, the

Americans, so Germans felt, stood by their friends when things got hot. And when the Wall came down, it was American President George H. W. Bush who did not hesitate for a minute to support German reunification in the face of reluctant European allies like Great Britain and France.

Finally, Germany was free, a sovereign state at last. Big Brother America was no longer needed for protection against the hungry Soviet bear. Relations remained warm throughout the 1990s. President Bill Clinton was well liked, and even when he led the way to stop atrocities in the Balkans with military means, Germany followed. For the first time since World War II, German soldiers participated in a war with their fighter-bombers. A small step for Americans, a gigantic step for Germans who could be convinced by their leaders in parliament only with the battle cry "No more Auschwitz"—meaning that the genocide in Kosovo had to be stopped at all costs, even if a taboo had to be broken—the ultimate taboo of postwar Germany: Don't go to war!

Germans were ready to defend themselves and their NATO allies against outside threats on their own territory, and they provided the largest army in Western Europe for this purpose till the end of the Cold War—but for this purpose only.

Only if you understand the magnitude of the decision to deviate from this path for the first time by joining the military action in the Balkans can you appreciate the next step, which came after September 11, 2001.

A quarter-million people congregated in front of the Brandenburg gate to show their support for America.

Nobody asked them to come. Germans understood that a friend was under attack and that help was needed. Chancellor Gerhard Schröder promised the United States "unlimited solidarity" in the fight against terrorism, and he delivered. A few months later, thousands of German soldiers moved to far-off Afghanistan, and they have been there ever since—a move completely unthinkable only a few years ago. By German standards, Chancellor Schröder had taken his fellow citizens extremely far with this commitment.

But U.S. President George W. Bush wanted more. And that is when things started to go very wrong.

President Bush, in the eyes of the Germans, committed the ultimate sin. He went to war again, this time against an enemy who quite obviously had neither intention nor means to attack the USA in any way. He went to war against Iraq.

There were no weapons of mass destruction, and Saddam Hussein had no intention of supporting the Islamic radicals of Al Qaeda, who ideologically threatened his Sunni-dominated regime as much as many other more or less secular Arab governments.

But Bush and his neocons wanted to crack down once and for all on the states that constituted his "axis of evil," and Iraq was to be only the beginning in his effort to bring U.S.-style democracy to the rest of the world.

Four thousand miles east of Washington, German chancellor Gerhard Schröder resisted this goal. In his fight for political survival in his 2002 election campaign, Schröder, who had risked a lot politically by sending troops to Afghanistan to help the USA in the fight against terrorism only months ago, now turned into an outspoken critic of Bush's war plans. This was very popular among German voters, and Schröder was able to turn around his fragile political fortune. He won the elections by a slim margin of just six thousand votes, with George W. Bush as his unwilling helper.

Never in the almost sixty years after WWII had U.S.-German relations reached such a weak point. Americans accused the Germans of being traitors and wimps, and Germans saw the Americans as reckless warmongers. Over the decades, America had gotten used to the idea that its German allies would fall in line eventually when it really counted. But this time, Schröder joined ranks with France and Russia against Washington's Iraq invasion. The White House was outraged. Secretary of Defense Donald Rumsfeld, his voice full of scorn, called this alliance "Old Europe," alienating Germans even further. The damage done back then is almost irreparable— despite the fact that both sides have done their utmost to bring working relations back to normal.

To the end of his term, George W. Bush stood for everything Germans despise. The violations of human rights are probably at the top of the list. Again and again, this president vetoed efforts to outlaw torture in the fight against terrorism, even against the advice of his own inner circle. He is also perceived as a man with his finger at the trigger of his gun, the proverbial American cowboy who shoots first and asks questions later, if he even bothers to ask questions at all. Mission accomplished—that was the Bush claim after U.S. troops overran Iraq. But Germans think that Bush's Iraq adventure did more damage to the American reputation around the globe than anything else, helping at the same time Al Qaeda to find more and more fighters for its cause not just in the Arab world but in Muslim quarters all over Europe, including Germany.

Germans don't want war. They have learned their lesson. After two disastrous world wars, Germans are at heart pacifists. Therefore they are allergic to the constant war cries emanating from Washington. First Afghanistan, then Iraq, now Iran?

Take the example of Afghanistan. Yes, American soldiers are dying in the dangerous south of that country. The U.S. administration is constantly pressuring the Germans to do more than they do already. Germans control the north of Afghanistan with thirty-five hundred troops, and they are good at that. They keep it relatively stable, with a mixture of mild military repression and a program to rebuild the civilian infrastructure. An extensive, long-term poll among Afghans has shown wide support for the German presence. About seventy-five percent say they want the Germans to stay.

The number of attacks in the north has doubled over the past year, and German soldiers are dying, too. Still, they are relatively lucky. Attacks in their sector constitute only three percent of the overall number of incidents. American, British, Canadian, and Dutch troops bear the brunt of the fight against the Taliban.

Still: when it comes to sending more German combat troops to the South, leaders in Berlin are reluctant to do more. About eighty percent of Germans are against it, and the German government will have a hard time overruling this prevailing sentiment.

Former Chancellor Helmut Kohl summed it up: "For a long time, they have accused us of getting into our combat boots too fast; now they accuse us of not getting into combat boots fast enough."

There is a yearning for change in the United States, not just inside the country but also over here, on this side of the Atlantic. Deep in our hearts, Germans want Americans to be their beloved role model again, someone to look up to—at the same time knowing quite well that the good old times of more or less blind trust will never come back. The old Atlanticists who took good relations for granted for many decades are fading away.

Reunited Germany has matured. A whole generation of young people sees no reason to depend on Big Brother America the way their parents and grandparents did.

They want to spend their vacation in Florida or California as they do in Spain or Italy, in a practically borderless European Union, and not be bothered by ill-tempered immigration officers enforcing ever-increasing security requirements at American airports. And they don't want to explain all the time to hostile Americans why Germany did not join the United States in the Iraq war.

Intellectuals in Germany hope that Americans will strive to recover their lost civil liberties, and that the citizens of the proverbial "land of the free" will eventually take back what the government took away from them. They see the pendulum swinging back in this direction.

Professionals in Berlin think tanks and bureaucrats in government offices also expect a change after the Bush administration ends. But they have no illusions: whoever conquers the White House after George W. Bush will keep the pressure on with calls for more burden-sharing in the global fight against terrorism, in the Middle East and other parts of the world. Radical Islam is the common challenge for many years to come, as is the need to stop proliferation of weapons of mass destruction.

But the most important demand is that any future U.S. administration steer away from unilateralism. If the USA wants more, then it must do more to bring its allies aboard. It's as simple as that.

There is a lot of room for improvement—that's for sure. But the debate about common values is not just empty talk. It may sometimes feel hollow, but a closer look confirms the obvious: the number of working democracies on this globe is limited, and Germany and the USA are certainly—and fortunately—in the same boat.

Germans are more than ready to give the relationship a second chance. Former Chancellor Helmut Schmidt summed it up nicely in a recent article: "Europe's faith in the United States may be shaken, yet we wish to maintain the transatlantic partnership. We want to be able to love America again, but we have become skeptical because for the past ten years, Washington has turned to us only when is has needed troops or money."

Schmidt laments at the same time the weaknesses of Europe. He makes the decisive point: "That is why we hope the new president will lead rationally and multilaterally—not least, we are convinced of America's vitality." It's fair to say that most Germans fully agree with this assessment.

The Truth about America

György Dragomán

America does not exist. America is Kansas, Kansas is the land of Oz. You can't really go there. No one can. It is just a fairy tale. America is farther than the moon. I know this is true, I am four years old, I am listening to the Wizard of Oz every day. It is my favorite story, my only double LP, my mother bought it for me on the black market, and therefore it is a big secret.

It's 1977, Transylvania, western part of Romania. The country is one of the more brutal places behind the Iron Curtain, with an atmosphere of fear resembling that of Stalinism. The Hungarian minority, to which I belong, is politically suspect, and therefore our situation is even worse. My parents do not get passports, not even to the friendly neighboring socialist republic of Hungary. I won't be allowed to leave Romania until I'm fifteen, and then I'll leave it for good, as our family will immigrate to Hungary.

All this lies well ahead in the future, and I am not even aware of our situation. I am living the life of a four-year-old—life is a big game—and so I do not even flinch when one day my father tells me never to repeat anything I hear at home outside our apartment. The next day we are supposed to talk about our favorite tales in the kindergarten. I ask him about the Wizard of Oz, my father tells me I should keep it secret. So I do, I tell the kindergarten teacher that my favorite tale is John and the seven-headed dragon.

America is the filthy cradle of imperialist capitalism; people there don't have the right to work. People starve in America. America is evil. Or so the kindergarten teacher tells us. I know this is not true, when my father told me about keeping Oz a secret he also told me that nothing they'd tell me in kindergarten would be true. The kindergarten teacher tells us we have the right to work, everybody in our socialist republic has the right to work. She tells us we don't realize how lucky we are that we were born here and not in America or the West. I am six years old. I know America does in fact exist, but it is still farther than the moon. I know America is the land of the free. America is not the West, it is something even better, it is the Wild West, where the buffalo roam free. I want to go there. I want to become a cowboy. Or even better, I want to become an Indian. I know going there is impossible, but I don't really know why.

The game we are playing has lots of rules; most of the rules have no explanation. And sometimes I forget them.

One day the kindergarten teacher asks me to recite the points of the compass. "North, east, south, west, and the Wild West." "What did you just say?" "The Wild West." "Oh the Wild West." "Yes the wild west. America." "Where did you hear about that, my child?" "At home."

"Who told you about the Wild West?" "Karl May." "What did you just say? Karl Marx?" "No, Karl May." "Who is Karl May?" Karl May is my favorite writer. I don't tell this to the kindergarten teacher. I cannot read, but he is still my favorite writer, my mother reads me all his books. I want to become an Indian as he did. We'll be having a carnival in our kindergarten, and I'll come dressed up as an Indian. This I do tell the kindergarten teacher. The kindergarten teacher tells me I am not supposed to. I am supposed to come dressed as a worker. "We all are going to dress up like workers." "No I am not. Workers are boring. They just work, I want to dress up like an Indian." I am not telling the kindergarten teacher that I have my own costume. My father even gave me a bear claw as a talisman. He told me it came from America, it was a claw of a real grizzly. I will wear it round my neck. Workers don't have talismans. "Workers are not working; they are fighting for peace." "Fighting for peace is boring. I am not going to fight for peace, I am going to fight with the Indians. With Winnettou. I am going to the Wild West. I am going to America." The kindergarten lady tells me to shut up.

The next day my parents are called into the kindergarten. They learn I committed a grave sin; I am a cosmopolitan, aping Western values. They should know better than to teach me such nonsense. Nonsense like Karl May. Nonsense like Indians. Nonsense like America. And they should know there is no way she will allow me to dress like an Indian. All the children are going to dress like workers. Or miners. Or tractor drivers.

No they are not. My mother smiles, reaches into her bag, and hands the kindergarten lady a soap. "Take this small gift, it's really nothing." I know this is what you are supposed to say when you bribe someone, this is one of the rules I have learnt. I also know it is a lie, as the gift is never a gift, nor is it ever small. My mother tells the kindergarten teacher she should not make a big deal of this Indian business. She knows how kids are. The kindergarten lady looks at the soap, she even smells it through the packing. The soap is Rexona brand. It smells like roses. You cannot get it in the shops. It is made in West Germany. My mother tells the kindergarten lady Karl May is East German. All the Indians in his books are friendly socialist Indians. The East Germans have even made movies out of his works. The Wild West is in fact in Yugoslavia. Winnettou the Apache chieftain, he is in fact Yugoslav, more precisely a Serb. His name is Gojko Mitic. I know this is a lie. The Wild West is in America. Winnettou is an Apache. And if not an Apache than West German, or if not West German than French, because in the West German movies he is played by Pierre Brice.

The kindergarten teacher puts the soap away. She tells my mother I may dress up as an Indian after all. My mother nods.

The carnival is next week. I don't speak English. I don't speak German. I don't speak any language but Hungarian. I also can recite three long sentences in Romanian, I have no idea about what they mean, but the kindergarten teacher spent long hours teaching these sentences to me. She told me that was the price for allowing me to wear my Indian costume. I think of the soap, I know she is lying, the soap was the price, and my mother paid it already. But I know I am supposed to pretend she did not, so I learn the sentences. I don't understand a word, but I learn them. My father made me a bow of layered wood, and a quiver made of real leather, and real feathered arrows, he made me a headband with feathers, he gave me a leather string for the bear claw. I want to wear all this; I really really want to become an Indian. So I am doing my best, diligently learning those sentences.

The day before the carnival we have a costume rehearsal. All the other kindergarten teachers of our county come to visit our kindergarten. Our kindergarten teacher tells me they have all come to see me in my costume; they want to see me dressed up as an Indian. I believe her. She tells me to stand on a pedestal; she tells me to recite the sentences she taught me. I do. I don't understand a word of it, I have no idea what I am saying. It is in Romanian, our kindergarten is a kindergarten for the children of the Hungarian minority. I know only a few words in Romanian. None of those are mentioned in the sentences I was made to learn. But I recite everything without a single mistake. It is a great success, everybody claps, especially all the other kindergarten teachers. They clap for minutes. I am delighted, I smile, I am waving at them. They clap some more. I think they clap because I am so clever. The next day I am allowed to wear my costume; I am allowed to be an Indian, the carnival is a great success. Everybody wants to touch the bear claw, but I am guarding it with my bowie knife, which is made of wood, with a blade covered in tinfoil.

A few years pass. I go to school. I learn Romanian. One day, I find the bear claw in a drawer. It is somewhat smaller than I remembered. But it still looks dangerous, its curved point sharp like a blade. As I touch it, I remember the carnival, and I remember the sentences I recited the day before standing on that pedestal. Suddenly I understand them. The past gets rewritten in a moment. Pride turns to shame. I realize I thanked the leader of the Socialist Party and his wife for being better parents than my real parents, I also thanked them for their tireless fight for peace, and in the last sentences I denounced the West, imperialism, and the United States. I was displayed as a model of patriotic education. I look at the bear claw. I know it was all a lie. I know it is not the claw of a real grizzly. I hide it somewhere, I never find it again.

I am nine years old, I begin learning English. I learn about Britain, I learn about America. I learn about Trafalgar Square and the Empire State building. I still don't think these places actually exist. I don't believe America exists. I know it does, but I still don't believe it. Karl May is still my favorite writer; I have read his books countless times. I know that those are indeed German books, written in German, and it is debated whether the author, Karl May, has ever set foot on the American continent, and even if he did, it is highly unlikely that he really earned the moniker of Old Shatterhand while becoming a blood-brother to an Apache chieftain and slaying grizzlies in close combat with the aid of a bowie knife. I have also learned that very few of his works are translated into English, he is virtually unknown and unread in the United States. This I find hard to believe. I still want to become an Indian. I know the Wild West does not exist any more. But I am planning to go there anyway.

I am twelve. I speak some English. America is real. Of this I am sure. I have got proof. America is a skewer. A black skewer made of twisted wrought iron. I am not allowed to touch it, it is one of my father's treasures, it hangs on the wall of our living room along with some of his other treasures, an old gunpowder horn, a hunting knife made of the sword my grandfather carried as a reserve officer. The skewer is a baroque piece of kitchen equipment; it dates back to the sixteenth century. It is ideal for roasting meat over an open fire. Or so my father tells us. But I know that is not the truth. Or not the whole truth. The skewer is much more. It is America, the United States. Or a secret link to it. I know. I know how to use it. I have seen my father do it one night. But I don't dare to do it.

One day I am at home alone. I can't go to school because I broke my ankle when we were playing a war game on a building site and I fell into a ditch and have to spend a few days in bed until the plaster on my leg hardens. I am reading *Moby Dick* by Herman Melville. I like it, but I am bored. I think of America, the New World, the whalers in their ships. I have no plans of going to sea, but I decide to look into this America business. I want proof once and for all. I get up from my bed, hobble into the living room, get our old East German WEF radio off the windowsill. The collapsible fish-rod antenna of the radio has been missing forever; it was ripped out of its socket. I get the radio, carry it into my room, and place it on the chair by the bed. Then I hobble back into the living room for the skewer. I hesitate before taking it off the wall, but in the end I do it. The skewer is huge and heavy; it is cold to the touch. I carry it back to my room. I saw my father do this only once, at night, through the crack of the door, but the image was unforgettable, so I know what to do.

I put the radio on my bed, I think of the whalers, the skewer is now a harpoon, I am going to catch America with it. I take a deep breath, and then I jam the skewer into the radio, right into the black hole in the plastic, where the old antenna used to be. I turn on the radio, switch the wave switch to the short-wave position, and begin slowly turning the search knob. The room is suddenly filled with the cracking hum of static, I am turning the search knob slowly, ever so slowly, listening to the fast unintelligible beep of Morse code, the whooping sound of stations coming into focus and disappearing again. I am looking at the red dial—there, behind the smudged Plexiglas, it creeps from right to left, and then suddenly I hear a faint voice proclaim that I am listening to the Voice of America. My hand tightens around the skewer, my body becomes a part of the antenna, the voice gets stronger, I am one with the radio, I know that the radio waves are passing through my body, I am listening to that distant American voice, most of the words I don't even understand, but it does not matter, only America matters. I am a hero, I am a spy,

I am doing something secret and forbidden, I am fighting the system from within, with a skewer and a broken radio. I am proud of myself, thrilled by my courage. I think of war movies and the French resistance.

I am so absorbed in this game, I don't even hear the key turn in the lock of our apartment, I don't hear my father arrive. I just hear his voice and look up, and suddenly there he is standing in front of my bed, asking me what I am doing. I let go of the skewer, the Voice of America fades back into the murmur of the static, I am back in our apartment, back in Romania, back behind the Iron Curtain.

My father grabs the skewer, pulls it out of the radio. He wants to know what I am doing. He does not seem to be very angry, just tense. I tell him I am sorry, I did not want to do anything wrong, I just wanted to find out the truth about America. My father nods, then asks me what do I care about America, don't we have enough trouble as it is?

I don't know what to answer, I am not even sure if he wants an answer at all. My father is not a hot-tempered man, but it is no use making him angry. So I counter with a question, I ask him about the bear claw, I ask him if it was a real grizzly claw or not. He sighs. That's the only answer. Then he sits beside me on the bed, still holding the skewer, its sharp point nested between two floorboards.

The radio is still on, the static is a low hiss. My father does not turn it off, he listens to it for a while, meanwhile, he puts his hand on the top of the radio in an awkward, gentle gesture, his fingers are touching the cracks in the plastic around the socket.

He asks me about the radio. He wants to know how did I think it got broken. The radio is old, it has always been broken. I tell him I have no idea, then I tell him, perhaps the security police did it, they mutilated our radio, to make listening to foreign broadcasts impossible.

My father smiles, he tells me he always knew I had a vivid imagination. Actually it was my grandfather who broke the radio. He grabbed the antenna and flung the radio against the wall. This happened in sixty-eight. Five years before I was born. It happened because of the events in Czechoslovakia.

I have no idea about Czechoslovakia. I have seen some cartoons that were made there, and someone once brought me a chocolate bar as a present, which was also from there, but that's all I know. My ignorance must be obvious, my father smiles at me, and then he tells me that if I really want to find out the truth about America, then I first need to learn about Czechoslovakia and about sixty-eight, about Hungary and about fifty-six, about Yalta and about forty-five.

It sounds like a lot of learning, but the tense way my father talks about all those countries and numbers makes me want to learn anyway. But first I have to ask him about my grandfather, about why he broke the radio.

My father tells me he broke the radio because the Americans did not come, it was the third time they did not come, and my grandfather had had enough. They did not come in forty-five, they did not come in fifty-six, and when they did not come in sixty-eight he suddenly had had enough, he did not want to listen to their voice anymore because he realized that they'd never come, and they'll never bring what they have promised, and we'll be stuck with what we have got for good and all.

My father's voice is raspy with tension, he tells me about the Hungarian revolution, which they listened to on the radio, not the WEF, back then they had an old transistor radio, and the Americans were promising help, and they'd promise they'd come and bring weapons, they'd promised they protect us from the Soviets, now that the Hungarian people have gone and decided it's time to take fate into their own hands.

He tells me about how people were waiting for the Americans to come ever since after the Second World War, he talks about the rumors of American soldiers having been sighted in the mountains, where they were preparing the ground for the rest of the troops. He tells me how he believed they must have been there even though he knew it could not have been true. He does not explain it further, but this sort of blind belief I understand fully. It is the way I believed in the grizzly claw, the way I believed in the Wild West.

My father's fingers are still caressing the cracks in the plastic. For a while he does not speak, and then he tells me that when the Russian tanks rolled into Budapest in November of fifty-six, my grandfather was weeping in front of the radio. That was the first time he saw his father cry.

The static is still humming; my father suddenly lets go of the antenna-hole and switches off the radio. He tells me that these are old stories, but our world is defined by old stories such as these, and even though he is my father, and fathers should always know better, he can't tell me the truth about America because he has never been there, and it is very likely that he won't ever have the chance to go there. He then gets up from the bed, takes the radio and the skewer, and walks out of the room.

I am lying on the bed, I put one hand on the plaster of my leg; my palm is all sweaty; the plaster is cool against it. I think of my grandfather's tears, the grizzly claw, the skewer, the Land of Oz, Czechoslovakia, tanks, and chocolate.

The door opens once again; my father comes back into my room with a book. It is a small gray volume. Before handing it over to me, he tells me that it might perhaps hold some of the truth about America. He tells me this was the book his own father gave him, when he asked him why he was crying. My grandfather told him that he was crying because he realized that the book, which he believed to be true, was in fact just a fairy tale. He was crying because he realized that the country he believed to have been built on that book, turned out to be just a fairy tale. He cried because he realized that the America he believed in did not exist, we'll never go there, and it'll never come to us.

My father finishes the sentence and shrugs; then he points at the book and tells me I should read it and judge for myself. Who knows, perhaps I will choose to believe in it, even knowing that it is just a fairy tale. Because we all have to believe in something, and it might as well be this book.

The book is dusty, even without opening it I can see that the pages are yellowed, the cheap paper has oxidized badly. I open the book; it is *On Liberty* by John Stuart Mill. I start to read it; it seems quite simple, but even as I am reading it I suspect that I don't fully understand it, and I am afraid I'll never find the truth about America.

In Praise of the Delinquent Hero, or How Hollywood Creates Terrorists

Sunny Singh

Many years ago, when the world was supposedly a better, more innocent place, I watched a pirated VHS copy of *Rambo III*, a trite but internationally successful film dedicated to "the gallant people of Afghanistan." I still remember the scene where an admiring Stallone hears the "rebels" explain their fight as a "holy war" against illegal and brutal occupation. One friend—from a Middle Eastern country long since engulfed by flames of war—excitedly pointed out that Rambo was helping, and being helped by, the *fidayee*—Islamic martyr/warriors—a word that few of us had heard before. "That's why he is a hero!" he declared excitedly, over and over again in the following weeks.

In the ensuing years, I have encountered Rambo heroically decimating opposition on flickering television screens in places as far afield as Peruvian jungles, the African bush, and Middle Eastern *souks*. James Bond, Terminator, and Rocky all remain favorite idols of America-"haters" as varied as Sudanese militiamen, Afghan warlords, and Hezbollah fighters. Go out farther into the jungle or the desert and you will find old grainy copies of classic Hollywood war films in the oddest of places.

"You desire what you see" is the cryptic clue handed by Dr. Hannibal Lecter to Agent Clarice Starling in the 1991 thriller *The Silence of the Lambs*. Given the information-rich contemporary culture that consistently bombards us with images, sounds, and ideas, we often overlook the ways that our desires are formed and transformed, often to reflect, refract, and repeat ancient stories of love, jealousy, envy, and hate. In a world with a surfeit of mass media, we ignore Dr. Lecter's warning at our own peril; if we desire what we see, then we desire what we see most often: commodities, heroes, and ideals.

Like the American military, the American film and television industry far outclasses the rest of the world in terms of size, budget, and reach. This is why it is Hollywood that creates the image of America that most of the world accepts. More important, Hollywood also hands the world the ideological lessons and values that often drive attacks and expose America to accusations of hypocrisy. Much of the world sees what Hollywood has long shown it—that what we desire can be achieved by individual effort, if necessary by violence, and that our delinquency shall be glorious (and in turn, desirable) if it can only be sufficiently heroic.

And make no mistake; the Hollywood hero has long been a delinquent. Living by his own rules, which often pit him against the state and society, the American hero, in much of the world, is still the lone cowboy—Henry Fonda on a horse, Sylvester Stallone in a jeep, or Will Smith in a spacecraft—who rides in to challenge and overthrow an oppressive, tyrannical authority.

More important, according to Hollywood's own rules, this lone cowboy is a delinquent outside the rule of law and the mores of society, driven only by his terrible, violent ethos and reliant only on his ability to wield the gun. Every American hero the world loves to watch and cheer—from Arnold Schwarzenegger's character in *Terminator 2* to Bruce Willis's in *Die Hard*—is someone just one shade beyond legality and beyond the control of a heartless, if not corrupt, state. And thanks to Hollywood's overwhelming reach, this hypermacho, independent, walk-the-edge, American hero is also the role model for millions who would like a share of the freedom and justice that Hollywood tells us is our right as human beings.

From Gaza to northern Nigeria, and from the banks of the Amazon to Bombay, storytelling in the twenty-first century is done with the moving image—celluloid, television, and digital cameras are ubiquitous across the globe. And they throw up interesting possibilities to enjoy, admire, desire, and imitate. Even in foreign markets dominated by Hollywood, the images refer to and build upon archetypes, endlessly re-creating, distorting, and transforming ideals and models to fit contemporary realities and possible futures. Thus, the images produced and packaged by Hollywood as paragons of the "American dream" are endlessly recycled and reinterpreted by viewers to match their own realities and experiences—often with wildly divergent results. This is why Hollywood's global reach, coupled with the variety of ways cinema is interpreted, makes for a potentially explosive mix.

For nearly a century, as the world's preeminent entertainment industry, Hollywood has not only sold American culture but also American products around the world. As early as the 1920s, savvy marketing professionals began introducing their products onto movie sets. Department stores marketed copies of clothes worn by stars in the films while car manufacturers scrambled to have their four-wheelers showcased on celluloid. Soon enough, Hollywood was selling the best of American typewriters, Levi's jeans, and toasters to the whole world. Along the way, the industry also began selling assault rifles, Stinger missiles, F-16s, and Apache helicopters. Who could resist the power of American weaponry, especially when wielded with the invincible might of a Hollywood action hero?

Alongside the products, perhaps unwittingly, and for just as long, Hollywood has also been selling a set of glamorously packaged cultural values. In innumerable cinematic tales starring the classic Hollywood delinquent-hero, these values are easily identified by their intrinsic distrust of sociopolitical institutions and officials, the privileging of individual judgment over the status quo, and finally, the utility of violent force in achieving goals, even if it means going beyond the pale of law. More important, however, this hero's muscles ripple in dissent against an oppressive, destructive state. From Hollywood we know that "evil" empires expand their might by oppressing and destroying "innocent" populations. In the globally successful *Star Wars* series, the "evil" empire is marked by its ability to destroy entire planets from great distances and with utter impunity. In the 1996 sci-fi thriller *Independence Day*, enemy aliens demonstrate their ability to not only surround earth with innumerable fighter crafts but also to cause immense damage from a great distance. Indeed, the war machinery is itself often the marker of "evil," with tanks rolling in large numbers to terrify and destroy innumerable civilians until, of course, a lone hero (perhaps aided by a rag-tag army) arrives on the scene.

Is it any surprise, then, that in the world beyond cinema it is America's massive war machinery that stands in for the "evil empire"? After all, to an illiterate Afghan peasant, Russian helicopters are little different from American Apaches while they send down showers of death that cannot be countered by small handheld weapons. Is it any surprise that when the average non-American sees sprawling military complexes manned by men with little cultural sensitivity but driving armored Hummers and armed with far too much firepower, they see the perfect Hollywood embodiment of evil?

Isn't it Hollywood that taught the world that "heroes" learn the local language, talk to children, are kind to women, and respect another's culture? After all, Hollywood taught us that "good" Indiana Jones has Arab friends and doesn't disrespect or attempt to rape local women. That particular offense is left for those from "evil" empires. In films ranging from western to sci-fi to war, Hollywood has taught us that it was only "evil" empires that held captives and tortured prisoners. For years, we knew that Clint Eastwood, Harrison Ford, and Sylvester Stallone stood for truth and justice even as they were tortured by bad guys wearing indistinguishable uniforms and running dingy prison complexes in dusty, far-off lands. Now, of course, it is the Americans who run similar prison complexes that administer electric shocks and beatings, or kill inmates at random. *Schindler's List* perhaps? Therefore, should it be a surprise that the Iraqis, Afghans, Lebanese, Somalians, or Venezuelans now identify America as the cruel empire that must be fought and defeated?

Hollywood taught us the difference between good and evil for years. But now America—drunk on its military and economic strength—is the evil empire. Why should America be surprised that the world does what Hollywood has taught us to do? After all, it was America's film industry that taught us that individual desire, motivation, and judgment—culminating in violence—was an appropriate, even ideal, response to the corrupt, decadent, tyrannical authority. Whether through Clint Eastwood in *The Pale Rider* or Robert De Niro in *Godfather II* or Sylvester Stallone with the supportive *jihadis* in *Rambo III*, Hollywood taught us that the only way to react was to take up weapons against injustice.

Action films are Hollywood's most popular export genre, as these rely the least on linguistic communication.

They provide justification for destabilizing violence by the delinquent hero, privileging the view from the criminal, albeit individualistic, margins against the powers of a state that argues for a monopoly on violence as a form of maintaining "peace." Not surprisingly, it is a reckless James Dean in *Rebel Without a Cause* or a righteous Marlon Brando in *Mutiny on the Bounty* or a tech-whiz-on-the-run Tom Cruise in *Minority Report* who features as hero. Across the decades, films declare that individual action, even though violent, is appropriate, necessary, and desirable.

In Hollywood or the real world, stories turn on points of view, making one man's hero into another's villain. This holds true for the Hollywood hero who may be cloaked in righteousness while his actions are essentially a quest to overthrow a current state structure, and then its replacement by another one. His quest for power leads him to provide constant provocation, intrusion, attack, and ambush of the government's forces. In each instance of apparent ambush of the heroic party, we need only shift our focus to realize that it is the Hollywood hero who inserts himself and his party into stable territories and forces a destabilization through acts of violence.

Such an idealization of delinquent violence of course raises the question: given that the most spectacular attacks against and in the West—9/11 as well as the Madrid and London train bombings—have been conducted by young men who were familiar with and apparently well assimilated into the popular culture of our times, can Hollywood's idealization of the delinquent hero be a factor informing their behavior? What other conclusion can be drawn when a tech-savvy cyber-*jihadi* chooses the codename of *Irhabi*-007 (terrorist 007) in tribute to his hero, James Bond? When young fighters in Afghanistan shyly admit to admiring *Rambo* and *Terminator*, or when *Harry Potter* sells millions of copies and tickets beyond the Western world, should we not question whether the ideals embodied by the delinquent hero are now "universal" and not culturally specific to America?

After all, the Hollywood hero taught us that violence was justifiable against a terrible oppressive state. He also taught us that only people on his side—the marginalized, the powerless, the oppressed—are innocent. Those with massive weaponry, innumerable tanks, and fighter planes are neither innocent nor worthy of compassion when facing homemade Molotovs and small arms. Why is it a surprise then that those whose homes are bombed from the American mile-high supersonic club are not particularly sympathetic about the 9/11 casualties? Wasn't it Hollywood that taught us that only those close to the hero are important? That only those who speak his language, love him, or are loved by him are to be mourned. All other civilian casualties are merely faceless, nameless "collateral damage." Why should Americans be shocked when that same standard is applied by much of the Middle East to the 9/11 dead?

Is it so ridiculous to reimagine Somalians fighting American Marines in similar weak-but-heroic terms? While a post-traumatic *Black Hawk Down* (2002) imagined Americans as victims of a numerically superior

Somalian militia, audiences in even a pro-American society like India cheered at the moment when the technologically superior U.S. Black Hawk was brought down by small arms. The world knew—from innumerable earlier Hollywood films—that guys in big helicopters with heavy weaponry are *always* bad. After all, that's what we had learned from Hollywood macho men dating back to John Wayne and Jimmy Cagney and from more recent incarnations like Will Smith and Tom Cruise.

One of the biggest Hollywood blockbusters of the past decade, Peter Jackson's *The Lord of the Rings*, based on the trilogy of novels by J. R. R. Tolkien, provides examples of the problems of such idealization of delinquent violence. We need look no further than the hijackers of the four planes of 9/11, men trained and educated in Western Europe and America who hoped they could strike at the heart of what they believed was the "evil empire." That motley group from Saudi Arabia—a closer human equivalent to what Tolkien described as an "unobtrusive but very ancient people" could not be imagined. Did the hijackers of 9/11 also see themselves as a "little people" too weak to go against the empire but still determined to see the attack through? Did they believe that they must continue against all odds because that is what "people in great stories do"? Did their courage falter at the thought of making their way deep into Mordor, and did a friend help sustain their courage?

We shall never know, mostly because few in America are willing or able to challenge with their imaginations what has become the overwhelmingly one-sided narrative of that tragic event. But one wonders whether others in the Middle East or Africa or Latin America also watch the epic trilogy and imagine themselves as a "little people" taking on the might of an evil empire?

Another of Hollywood's favorite heroic types is that of the hero-in-disguise or the king-in-exile. *Batman* and other superhero sagas rely on our instinctive sympathy for the hero who must live in the shadows, biding his time and working for "justice and peace" in the face of ridicule, anonymity, and opposition. Aragorn of *The Lord of the Rings* and *Spiderman* are popular contemporary examples of this type. Indeed the latest *Spiderman* film even takes on the issues of excess violence and subsequent media vilification for the hero-in-disguise. Yet from a slightly different perspective, this hero is once again a violent delinquent fighting for the overthrow of the current oppressive state and the restoration of a supposedly just realm. More important, regardless of his apparent social standing or indeed age, it is this hero-in-disguise who knows better than the oppressive brutal state! And at the right time, his truth and glory shall be revealed, while the state shall be undermined and humiliated in turn.

Hollywood doesn't just present the hero-in-disguise in numerous comic-linked products but also casts him or her as the just avenger or representative in most films of the action/war genres. Arnold Schwarzenegger's career has been built on a series of films starring him as the lone savior fighting all odds—and disbelief—to bring peace and justice. Harry Potter is snubbed by his friends, vilified by the media, and pursued by the government, but his heroism requires him to stand by his own judgment. He endures all his troubles until age and experience enable him to finally confront and defeat the "evil" Voldemort. A young Palestinian child—walking past American-financed tanks—finds a bit more than just fantasy in this tale.

More perilously, the exiled king returning to restore a just kingdom is not so distant from ideals of the *Mahdi*, the "hidden imam" of the Shi'ites, or a return to the Caliphate. Most Americans—out of ignorance or hubris—ignored the frightening news clip of Mullah Omar appearing before his followers in Prophet Mohammad's robes. Yet the message implicit in that act went out loud and clear to the Taliban. Similarly, the Iranian president Ahmadinejad's repeated reference to the *Mahdi* is meant to invoke the possibility of the very imminent return of a hidden king who shall restore power and glory to an apparently oppressed people. In the past decade of U.S. imperial ventures, this particular ideal seems to have gained strength, finding expression among militants and those who oppose the USA around the world.

Under Nasrallah's leadership, the Hezbollah has moved to occupy center stage in the past few years. Not inexplicably then, while Western powers (cast here as the "evil empire") eye the Hezbollah as terrible opponents, the Lebanese have been receiving proof of the group's capacity for "justice" and "peace." The Hezbollah runs hospitals and schools and rebuilds homes and roads, as it did after the 2006 U.S.-sanctioned Israeli bombings; civic services form the bulk of the organization's activities, even as the Western press qualifies the group as "terrorists." Working from the position of the hero-in-disguise, Nasrallah, with his ability to elude western forces and his "sacrifice" of his own son to the cause, reinforces his legend among his constituents. These strengthen the group's position within Lebanon and help them to recruit not only soldiers and activists, but also cheerleaders and silent supporters, a strategy that served them well in the 2006 conflict with Israel. The organization has also constructed its military image based on the warrior-hero characteristics displayed by epic heroes of the same mold: stoicism, courage, and determination in the face of all odds have marked the Hezbollah's move from the shadows to its current popular position as the "justly anointed king." *Men in Black*? Or is it *Superman*? Or simply an aging Don Corleone weeping for the death of his son while simultaneously ordering vengeance?

A final Hollywood hero requires attention, in part because, since 9/11, he has become the greatest bogeyman of our times: the suicide warrior/martyr. Despite hysterical claims that somehow the suicide warrior is a specifically Muslim cultural phenomenon, Hollywood has spent more than five decades glorifying the ideal. Hollywood has produced heroic suicides in blockbusters as varied as *Aliens III* or *Terminator II*, and of course the current film adaptations of the *Harry Potter* books. Earlier examples would include war films ranging from *Stalag 17* and *Von Ryan's Express* to *The Guns of Navarone* and industry classics such as *Butch Cassidy and the Sundance Kid.* Many of these films may have faded from American memory, but pirated and grainy television prints continue to circulate in parts of the world far removed from American shores.

The suicide warrior/martyr is a complex phenomenon, as it relies on self-destruction as an assertion of empowerment. This allows the perpetrator to deal a psychologically (and possibly militarily) crippling blow to the enemy—an oppressive state and/or a rival population. The key to this archetype is not the necessary destruction of the hero, but the desire for self-destruction that motivates him/her. Perhaps because of the inherent paradox of this phenomenon, the suicide warrior/martyr is popular with people who see themselves as relatively powerless. Such a warrior/martyr not only achieves a blow against a seemingly invincible enemy but also inspires the rest of the population to continued resistance, thus fulfilling the key aim of heroic action.

In most narratives, the suicide warrior/martyr is depicted by twin strands, one that ends in death and destruction, and another—generally symbolic of a younger renewing generation—that ends in military success and life. Harry Potter must grow to battle Voldemort precisely because the self-sacrificing death of his mother bestows him with a special protection. Indeed, the final episode of this series poses an interesting challenge to America's, and Hollywood's, conception of suicide warriors (and bombers) as the young hero takes on what is, in reality, a suicide mission, dying in the process only to find redemption, renewed life, and invincibility from his enemies. Long before 9/11, in the popular Will Smith–starring *Independence Day*, an aging alcoholic pilot—played by Randy Quaid—prone to delusion finally achieves heroic redemption when he flies his craft kamikaze style into the belly of an alien spacecraft, thus finding the only way to damage the enemy. The act not only inspires other people on earth to do the same but also restores the lost respect and affection among his children.

The twin strands allow the narrative to retain an element of hope, although it is inevitably the narrative of suicide cloaked as self-sacrifice that resonates more strongly. One wonders whether the Westernized Saudi pilots steering the planes into the Twin Towers had found some encouragement from *Independence Day*, where heroic Americans must fly their crafts into the enemy to achieve immense destruction? Or had they grown up with the original *Star Wars* trilogy that similarly glorified the suicide missions undertaken by the militarily and numerically weaker "rebels" against the "evil empire"?

For over a century, Hollywood has peddled a quintessentially American set of cultural values to the world. Within America, this may have been meant to provide a necessary national narrative to explain, value, and exemplify certain facets and myths of history of the nation. However, once exported beyond American borders, these same values have provided the world with necessary lessons in dealing with brutal totalitarianism. Through its greatest blockbusters, Hollywood has taught us that we need not accept tyranny, that torture is wrong, and so is the occupation of foreign lands. It is Hollywood that taught us that evil empires are always identified by disproportionate power and indiscriminate use of military force. And it is Hollywood that taught us that all we need to overthrow tyranny is one lone warrior willing to take on the institutions of oppression with a judicious use of will power and ammunition.

Therefore, why should America be surprised that people beyond its shores, living in authoritarian military dictatorships or monarchies, with limited firepower, little to live for, and an immense sense of grievance, choose to emulate the Hollywood hero? It may well be argued that anti-American militants mounted on Toyota SUVs, AK-56s slung over their shoulders, Reeboks laced over their camouflage trousers, passion and determination simmering in their eyes, and a willingness to take on an irrational, oppressive, imperial state, are more "American" than those who care to fight under the Stars and Stripes. They are definitely better embodiments of Hollywood's all-American hero than the leering uniformed guards at Abu Ghraib or Washington's slimy *apparatchiks* who exonerate torture with complex legalese.

Dreams of a Revolution Baby

Zarah Ghahramani

Bombs and rockets rained down on Iranian cities all through my childhood. In Tehran and Kermanshah, where I grew up, I remember the bombs exploding with a splintering sound so loud that I would have been deafened if I hadn't pressed my hands tightly over my ears. Almost as hard on my ears as the bombs themselves was the scream of the air-raid alarm. When the siren sounded, I knew that I had to run to my mother, and my mother knew that she had to get my brothers and sisters and me down to the shelter within seconds. In the later years of the Iran-Iraq War (1980–1988), my family had its own air-raid shelter, but earlier we shared one with people from the neighborhood. While the bombs exploded overhead, old men and women sat with their lips moving soundlessly as they counted prayer beads. There was not much conversation down in the shelters, just a lot of shouting as mothers rounded up their kids. But one conversation I do recall made a deep impression on me. It went like this:

"It's not Saddam we're fighting. It's America."

"Brother, it's the truth."

"Americans give the Iraqis bombs and rockets. It's America, believe me."

"I know it, brother."

Children need heroes, but they also need villains. Up until I'd overheard this conversation, the great villain in my gallery of good people and bad people had been Saddam Hussein. I thought of him as a monster with huge, battering fists. His appetite for evil was so great that it had to be fed on blood each day. He would not rest until every Iranian, myself and all the dear members of my family included, were either dead or enslaved. And how could Saddam have escaped my hatred? The government exhorted all Iranians to pray for Saddam's death. His picture featured on giant billboards, looking not very like the salivating giant of my nightmares, but hideous enough with his lips curled into a sneer. But now came this strange new idea. Saddam was merely the servant of an even greater monster called America. Astonishing! I'd barely heard of America before this time, although I knew that it was a country a long way off across the blue parts of the atlas I'd seen at school.

It is fascinating to me to think back now to that first mention of America. How ready I was to accept this country I'd barely heard of as the source of all the misery and hardship around me! Perhaps that overheard conversation came at a moment when my imagination was craving more complexity. Perhaps, without realizing, I had exhausted my disgust with Saddam and craved a more mysterious foe. And then, of course, the status of this new enemy was reinforced in my mind by the government's fresh billboards depicting the skinny, top-hatted figure I came to know as Uncle Sam with his arm around a shorter, diminished Saddam. Whatever was going on in my mind to prepare me for hating distant America even more than nearby Iraq, it was also going on in the minds of millions of other Iranian schoolchildren.

By 1987, America was the enemy, *our* enemy, and we hated America with all the passion and intensity that small children reserve for the wicked. I even made myself believe that it was the mysterious, malevolent Americans who were responsible for taking the cartoons off the television. The Americans had somehow gained control of the set. Out of sheer spite, they denied me the enjoyment of watching animated figures bouncing around on the screen. It was actually the government that had pulled the cartoons, considering them too frivolous for a nation busy honoring the "martyrs" of the war, but I came to know that only later. I would sit watching the dingy fare offered in place of the beloved cartoons and mutter to myself, "Stupid Americans!" It was the same when I watched my mom fishing for coupons in her handbag, struggling to keep her place in the queue during the years of food rationing. Why were we eating such bland food? Why did we have to buy even rice with coupons? "Stupid Americans!" The war widows my mother and I came across in the streets when we were shopping—you could always tell a fresh widow by her haunted eyes— owed their wretched state to the wicked Americans.

The Iran-Iraq war (known tendentiously at the time of the fighting, and today, as the "Iraq-imposed war") concluded just before my eighth birthday. The fighting was as savage as in any war ever fought. Iraq introduced gas bombardment, used for the first time since World War I, and was able to rely on American state-of-the-art aerial weaponry unavailable to any other ally of the United States, with the exception of Israel. In this same war, Iran did some innovating of its own, demonstrating the crude effectiveness of clearing minefields by marching soldiers over them. The most reliable estimate of casualties on the Iranian side is five hundred thousand deaths, including civilians. Although a long-standing enmity between Saddam and the Iranian state grew out of what was seen as the oppression of Iraqi Shiites by Saddam's favored Sunni elite (Iran being, of course, overwhelmingly Shiite), Iranians saw the arming of Iraq by America as payback for the Tehran Embassy hostage crisis of 1979–1980. Saddam, hungry for both territory and glory in 1979, seized on the instability in Khomeini's newly declared Islamic Republic as an opportunity to attack. Once the war was over, all Iranians, including schoolchildren such as myself, were expected to reserve their special contempt for the role played by the United States in the conflict. Saddam was not quite forgiven, but he was represented more as a misguided brother-in-the-faith than a cold-blooded predator.

Although my childhood hatred of America came along suddenly, a great many Iranians far older than I had a long-standing contempt for the United States. These Iranians had grown up under the regime of Shah Mohammad Reza Pahlavi, an avid supporter of the United States who was in turn avidly supported by the United States. They did not remember the regime of the Shah with fondness.

His state security agency, SAVAK, had maintained a reign of terror over Iran for decades before the Shah's exile in 1979. He was seen as a stooge, a patsy, a man so besotted by the West and Western culture that he forgot how to love and protect his own country. He sold Iranian oil to Europe and the UK for peanuts and purchased weapons from the United States at hugely inflated prices. When I started high school, the role played by the United States in Iranian politics under the Shah was strongly emphasized in history classes. I can't even say that those in the Iranian regime charged with fashioning the high-school curriculum and its contents had to bend the truth much to produce the desired effect. In 1953, the CIA had organized the coup that deposed the nationalist Prime Minister Mohammad Mossadeq. The Shah, who had left Iran while Mossadeq was rousing nationalist sentiment among the populace, demanding a fair price for Iranian oil, was reinstalled on the Peacock Throne by the CIA. The Shah never forgot to whom he owed his position. Our history textbooks included the analysis of European and American journalists and academics in corroboration of the regime's argument, so there was little reason to feel skeptical. My entire generation of students, born after the triumph of the Islamic Revolution of 1979, went to high school with a foundation of grievances against the United States laid down during the Iran-Iraq War; it was on this foundation that we built our disdain.

During the decade following the end of the Iran-Iraq war, hating America became more complicated and required greater concentration. Life gradually became less of an ordeal. By 1992, people I knew were traveling abroad to Dubai and Turkey, even to Europe. They returned with American-made jeans and sneakers, and posters of the extraordinarily beautiful and amazing Michael Jackson. They also brought back videotapes, records, CDs, nearly all of them featuring American performers. It is impossible to deny that American popular culture is irresistible. My generation of Revolution Babies, in our early teens as of 1992, were in most respects as shallow as any generation of teenagers in the West, and we swooned. A pair of Lee jeans was as coveted as anything on earth among the kids I knew at that time. We couldn't wear the jeans out and about, but we could show them off behind the closed doors of our homes. I would imagine that strutting about in Lees was an experience very like (I would imagine) entering paradise along a path of rose petals to the chorusing of angels. It's commonplace to say that middle-class people all over the world own up to conflicting emotions over America. The crudeness of American foreign policy since the Second World War gradually drained away the goodwill that the United States built up over more than a century; however, only those with especially rarefied taste wanted to do without the lovely nonsense that America provided. Lovely nonsense you could wear, eat, view, listen to, drive, and fill your kitchen with.

But I have to say that for my generation of Iranians, there was no conflict. With a certain amount of reflection, we could distinguish between what we liked about America and what we loathed. I would guess that this is the same for people from most other countries. We were never in a position of having to hate ourselves for loving Lees and Michael Jackson while we said scathing things about what the Americans were doing in Palestine. The pleasure we took in owning American things was not a guilty pleasure. I don't think it would be out of line to say that I and other Iranians of my generation had come to understand, by our early teens, that America accommodated both people of terrible ill will and people who occupied themselves by turning out petty trifles that everybody loved. Our disdain for America was not ideological; we didn't think very long or very hard about commercial imperialism.

We had also grown more aware of the mixture of good, bad, and ugly in our own country. Among the patrons of the Iranian regime—those who owed their employment to the people in power—and away from the major cities, young men and women of my generation perhaps found little to complain about and a great deal to admire in the rigid ideology of Khomeini and his successors. But in the cities, girls like me and boys of the same age were maddened by the regime's nosiness. I found myself rolling my eyes and whispering swear words a hundred times a week as first one and then another of the regime's stooges got in my face. Hideous boys of the Basaj militia would hurry up to me in the street to check that I wasn't wearing lipstick or Blush-On. Or a car that I was traveling in with my friends would be pulled over at a roadblock so that these same kids could sniff our breath to make sure that we hadn't been drinking alcohol. We ran a gauntlet of humiliations every time we left our homes. I recall a woman stopping me on the sidewalk and hissing at me that I was dishonoring the blood of her son martyred in the war by allowing my headscarf to ride back, revealing an inch of fringe. More significant than our exasperation with these, perhaps petty, restrictions on our freedom was the increasingly great exception we took to the arrests of citizens who had spoken out against the curtailment of basic liberties, such as freedom of dissent. The people arrested—teachers, journalists, academics—were perfectly polite dissenters, after all, and as a matter of fact, I was no firebrand myself, nor were my friends. By the time my generation of urban middle-class Revolution Babies reached our late teens, we were fed up with the regime and had concluded that only maniacs and morons ever held the reins of power, in Iran or anywhere else.

In my first year of university in Tehran, I joined up with many thousands of students all over Iran to agitate for political reform. Our demands were mild enough: teachers should be free to exercise genuine disinterest in the classroom, instead of being required to promote the government's agenda; we also demanded that arrested dissenters should be freed. I didn't realize then what I have now come to understand: that ideologues cannot contemplate compromise of any sort, since compromise is seen—quite rightly—as a diminishment of authority.

I was snatched from the street one afternoon by state security agents, detained at Evin Prison in north Tehran, and over a period of weeks, made to regret that

I'd ever been born. The interrogations and torture were unrelenting and went far beyond anything I had imagined during the months of protest on the streets, when with foolish bravado I had believed myself capable of standing up to whatever could be inflicted on me in the event of arrest. I was freed only after I had signed a document in which I "confessed" to practically everything that had gone wrong in the world in my lifetime. In the years following my release, it became more and more evident to my family that, subdued though I was, I would one day slip up, allow my rage to gain control of me, and shout something desperate in the streets. When that happened, I would be rearrested, and perhaps not escape with my life this time. So it was arranged that I would leave Iran, and I did.

Leaving your native land on a holiday might be thrilling, but leaving for good makes you feel as if the thousand fine strands that bind your being have been severed with a single slash. I was eventually able to make a new home for myself thousands of miles from Iran, but I have had to accept that I will live my life with a part of me given over to a sorrow that cannot be soothed. Iran is my homeland. We are only ever granted one homeland, only one opportunity to love a place with the same passion that we love the greatest poetry.

Looking at Iran from the outside, I see as clearly as ever all the nonsense that fills the heads of the people there who hold power. But that is not what boils my blood. Regimes come and go, madmen eventually leave the stage and fail to return. What remains forever is Iran. I become something like a mad person myself when I see how vulgarly Iran is caricatured in the West. This broad land with thousands of years of history, a land of great variety and great sophistication is characterized as some sort of desert hellhole peopled entirely by homicidal cretins. Americans have been influenced to see Iran as I used to see Saddam Hussein: a vile monster with huge battering fists.

But I was seven years old when I conjured that monster.

As an adult, I understand America in a way that would, I think, be common among Western middle-class citizens outside the United States: as a monster, yes, but a strangely pied monster, capable of revealing, when the stage lighting is right, great charm. I admire America's institutions and wish with all my heart that my own country could boast of a genuinely disinterested judiciary, for instance; a truly free press; an uncorrupted franchise. But what upsets me—more than upsets me, what is abhorrent to me—is the ungovernable need of many Americans to think well of themselves in every circumstance. It's a prejudice that causes great harm.

How many images of Vietnamese peasants sorrowing beside burning villages did it take before a slender majority of Americans ceased to think that successive administrations were increasing the sum of human happiness with a program of incineration? Americans have come to represent to me—certainly to most Iranians, and probably to many millions of other world citizens—a people capable of forgiving themselves at the very moment of inflicting death and suffering on innocent people; instant self-absolution. This is quite an unusual sort of wickedness, last witnessed, I think, when Turks were murdering Armenians a century ago and absolving themselves by explaining that it was for the Armenians' own good, or, more recently, when the Nazis composed in advance their justification for mass murder of unspeakable vileness. I have more reason than most to detest the motives and methods of certain figures in the Iranian regime, so my disgust is worth listening to. My anti-Americanism, if it is to be called that, began in infantile caricature, but it was a caricature that powerful people in America seem cheerfully determined to render accurate.

The Land of the Long Submarine Sandwich

Tom Segev

The first thing I knew about America was that it had tremendous peanut butter. That was thanks to Aunt Clara's packages. She was the sister of my grandfather on my mother's side and emigrated in the 1920s from Germany to America. I never met her, but in the 1950s, when times were hard in Jerusalem, she sent us care packages.

My parents came to Palestine as refugees from Nazi Germany. My father was killed in the 1948 war in Jerusalem. My mother was left alone with two children and had a hard time making a living. Aunt Clara's packages were a real help—aside from peanut butter, they contained lots of other good things.

In Germany, my parents had been students at a famous art school, the Bauhaus, and like many of their friends, they were Communists. At some point during the 1950s, my mother dragged me to some street in Jerusalem for an anti-imperialist demonstration. I remember shouting "Foster-Dulles Go Home!" at the top of my lungs, without having a clue who he was. They told me he was a bad man, so it was difficult for me to believe that he came from the same country as Aunt Clara's peanut butter. Recently, when digging through an ancient leather suitcase full of family papers, I discovered that, after my father's death, Aunt Clara sent us all the documents we needed to immigrate to America. My mother never told me this. She is no longer alive, so I can't ask her why she stayed in Israel. My guess is that she might not have wanted to live in America for ideological reasons. Would I rather have grown up in America? I'm not sure.

Either way, my mother's ideology did not keep me from harboring my own American dream. That was thanks to other things Aunt Clara sent, like models of American farmhouses and an amazing device that took me to Manhattan long before I even knew what a television set was. It was called a View-Master, a kind of binoculars into which you inserted cardboard wheels of color slides that each produced a three-dimensional image. Thus, as a boy, I ascended to the top of the Empire State Building, crossed the Brooklyn Bridge, and sailed to the Statue of Liberty. When I first arrived in New York, in 1971, at the age of 26, I felt as if I were revisiting my childhood haunts.

Then Aunt Clara bought us a subscription to *National Geographic*. I don't know what impressed me more—the giant Sequoias in California, the Grand Canyon vistas and space missions covered by the magazine, or the certificate that arrived in a large, dark yellow envelope with the subscription. It was so official, so formal. I was inordinately proud to belong to the National Geographic Society. *National Geographic* encouraged me to learn to read English and also opened many other lands before me. But the whole world always looked to me like part of America. My best friend was Tom Sawyer.

My American dream was hardly exceptional. We all grew up in America. True, Israel, during its early years, was governed by a social-democratic party headed by David Ben-Gurion, who called himself a socialist. Some of the parties in his coalition governments identified with the "world peace camp" led by the Soviet Union. This was more than a political and ideological stance—it was also a cultural identity. Kibbutzniks sang Russian songs as if the songs were Israeli. A leader of one of those parties referred to the USSR. as his "second homeland."

The United States did not take Israel's prevailing socialist sentiment lightly. To counter it, America granted Israel a generous loan, which among other things helped to shore up Ben-Gurion's leadership. The USA also set up a special fund to influence Israeli culture. This organization distributed Hollywood westerns and Elvis Presley records; people who wanted to feel as though they knew the truth read *Time* magazine.

These efforts were not really necessary. After the Korean War, small countries had little choice but to affiliate with either the Eastern or Western bloc, and Ben-Gurion led Israel into the West. One of his reasons was the need and the opportunity to obtain the assistance of America's Jews. The Arab countries won the support of the Soviet Union, which persecuted its own Jewish citizens. Ben-Gurion's position thus seemed correct, and even though Eisenhower's America did not immediately stand by Israel, most Israelis—especially young Israelis—saw themselves as part of the world led by America. Instead of khaki shorts and sandals, we began hanging out in jeans and sneakers. There was nothing more fun than necking in Dad's car with Connie Francis songs playing on the radio.

To those looking back, what stands out is how little hostility America evoked, even among intellectuals who identified with the socialist left, even those who had grown up on kibbutzim. Intellectuals in other countries were much more antagonistic. At the beginning of the 1960s, a play called *I Like Mike* was staged in Tel Aviv. Written by Aharon Megged, it was about an Israeli mother who did everything she could to hunt down a Jewish boy from America to marry her daughter. Megged, then a leftist, wanted to make fun of how Israelis abnegated themselves in the face of everything that came from the United States. But over the years, the play underwent the same Americanization as Israeli society as a whole. In its film and musical-comedy versions, it was just cheerful, while the ideological satire that had been the trademark of the original version entirely vanished.

The deeper they plunged into the American sphere of influence, the more Israelis began to include America as part of their collective identity. Most Israelis view their country as one of the most dramatic success stories of the twentieth century; many see Israel's success as part of America's achievement. A popular myth has it that Israel won its independence in a heroic struggle against British rule, just like America. People from all over the world settled in Israel, and just as in America they were supposed to jump into the melting pot and emerge with a new national identity. Just like in America, they were supposed to head out to the frontier as pioneers and make it bloom. The story of the first Israelis is a story of great hope and faith that everything could only be better. It was the same fundamental assumption that powered the American dream.

At the same time, Israel committed itself to the principles of liberal democracy. Ben-Gurion instructed his foreign minister that "the state of Israel is not passive and neutral in the world's great debates: in the ideological debate it is democratic and anti-Communist." Therefore, relations between Israel and America could be based on what were endlessly termed their "shared values." Ben-Gurion, fantasizing that Israel would join NATO, forced Israelis to reconcile with West Germany.

Most Israelis viewed the Vietnam War as a test of the USA's willingness to protect its small allies, so they supported the war. Before launching the Six-Day War of 1967, Israel waited until it received a green light from Washington. Subsequently, opposition to the Vietnam War intensified in the USA, and Israelis internalized this change. America's antiwar protests manifested themselves in Israel as protests against the oppression of the Palestinians.

America's civil-rights struggle turned, in Israel, into a battle to end discrimination against Jews who came from Islamic countries; some of these Jews organized a movement that they called the Black Panthers. In the 1970s, a movement called Peace Now appeared. Several of its leaders had been born in the United States, while others were graduates of American universities.

Beginning in the 1980s, most Israelis began living an American lifestyle, continuing a process that had begun in the 1960s. Israel's first supermarket opened in Tel Aviv in the summer of 1958; the spring of 1960 saw the first commercial radio broadcasts. In the meantime, the first skyscrapers were built in Tel Aviv, one of which was the Hilton hotel. Immediately after, the Six-Day War television broadcasts commenced, and that same year the first bottles of Coca-Cola appeared in Israeli stores.

In contrast with Israel's founding ideology, most Israelis do not work in agriculture. They live in cities or, in many cases, in bedroom suburbs. People drive to work in their cars, spend most of their time in air-conditioned offices, in front of computers, exchanging e-mail and surfing the Internet bilingually, in Hebrew and in English. They go out for a quick lunch and, unlike their parents, eat their main meal of the day in the evening. They say "hi" when they arrive and "bye" when they go, rather than "*shalom*," as they once did. They can now buy their children *National Geographic*'s Hebrew edition.

Spending a few years in America, for study or work, has become an accepted and sometimes requisite part of the biography of the Israelis who comprise the elite in every field, including industry, the military, science, politics, and the media. Israeli high-tech companies aspire to and frequently succeed in raising capital on American stock exchanges. The country's most prominent economic newspaper has an English name—*The Marker.* Israelis follow the American news just as they do local news; they can cite American interest rates and NBA scores; they follow the presidential elections as if they were contests for prime minister of Israel.

When I first arrived in America, to pursue my doctorate at Boston University, I felt as if I were at the center of the world and, as one might expect, I suffered an acute case of culture shock. Everything seemed so powerful and so huge. Not only were the buildings higher and the submarine sandwiches longer than any building or sandwich I had ever seen before, but even the people were taller than in Israel.

Like many Israelis, I had a tendency to ridicule Americans for their shallowness. In our arrogance, we told ourselves that we Israelis came from a more just society. One evening, at the entrance to Tiffany's in New York, I spotted the first homeless man I had ever seen; Hebrew did not even have a word for such a person. Our condescension did not diminish our dream to be part of the American world. In the Harvard Library's reading room, I believed that I was in the best university library in the world, and at concerts of the Boston Symphony, I felt that I was hearing the best orchestra in the world. The *New York Times* was, and remains, in my opinion, the best newspaper in the world.

But the most profound experience I had during that period in America was not my university studies. Instead, it was following the daily progress of the Watergate scandal. I was infinitely impressed. I sat in front of the TV for hours, watching the strongest country in the world examine itself mercilessly, fearlessly, and impartially, in the spirit of its Constitution and of the foundations of democratic rule. Watergate affected an entire generation of Israelis who followed it as I did, and if I had to define America in a single word, it would not be Microsoft, not even Woody Allen—it would be Watergate.

Israeli democracy owes to America its courage to persevere in a hostile, fanatical, and benighted environment. Watergate taught us the importance of governmental transparency. The Israeli Supreme Court has fortified its position at the inspiration of the American Supreme Court and has bestowed on Israeli society the fundamental values of freedom and civil rights that were forged in America. Individualism came from America, as did the value of tolerance: Like American society, Israeli society is not free of discrimination and injustice, but, under the influence of America, Israelis have learned to treat women and minorities more fairly, and to respect the Other in a multicultural society. The fact that so many millions of Americans were offered the opportunity to choose between a woman and a black candidate for the Democratic presidential nomination demonstrates, for me, American society's commendable ability to translate into political reality what was only a short time ago simply "politically correct."

Not everything that has come from America is good, and not everything American gets extolled in Israel. An important Israeli journalist who spent several years in the United States, Nahum Barnea, wrote of Michael Moore:

His film, *Fahrenheit 9/11*, is an unhealthy mixture of facts, lies, and demagogy. He has won fame in Europe only because the current fad in Europe is to hate Bush, with or without connection to the facts. He has made a splash in the United States for a similar reason. Only a few journalists of antlike diligence have bothered to check out the truth of the factual statements in the film. They found lots of holes.

As one might expect, Michael Moore is already here in Israel. Michael Moore is here because we adopt everything that comes from America, good or bad. He is here because people are running away from the bother that real journalism involves.

Likewise, enthusiasm about America's economic system has translated itself into a loss of the social solidarity that was once one of Israel's trademarks. The privatization of social services, a development influenced by the economic theories of Milton Friedman, has exacerbated economic disparity.

As Israel has become more American, Israelis have also learned to marvel at America's great failures. How could it not have known how to defend itself against the terrorists who obliterated the World Trade Center? How could a space shuttle like the Columbia have crashed? How could Americans have treated a disaster-plagued city like New Orleans as they have? How could they have elected (and reelected) a man like Bush? How did they fail in Iraq?

More and more Israelis are beginning to sense that the United States is in decline. They interpret the rise of China and India and the recession in the USA as historical evidence of that decline, just as the Communist and British empires declined before it, and countless other empires before them. Israelis track the dollar's descent assiduously. As it continues to weaken, America's prestige depreciates as well.

Even so, most Israelis see American support of their country—including billions of dollars of military and economic aid—as axiomatic. They are aware that, to a large extent, they live at the expense of the American taxpayer; they assume that it is in the interests of the United States to fund them. Some groups in America have, over the years, lent support to the Israeli peace movement; others have funded Israel's settlements in the occupied territories, and large sums are poured into Israel to inculcate neoconservative discourse. But when Americans talk about "support for Israel" in America, they mean that they will not impose a policy different from that determined by the Israeli government. *Israel* means, without exception, *the Israeli government.*

Given all we have received from America over the years, given all we have learned from it, it seems to me that we have good reason to point out that America has missed a historic opportunity. America should have done more to prevent us from making the mistakes we have made, especially following the Six-Day War. Transcripts of Israeli cabinet meetings, classified until recently, indicate that had the United States insisted that Israel not annex East Jerusalem after its conquest in 1967, then Israel would have refrained from doing so. That annexation has shown itself to be a principal obstacle to peace between Israel and the Palestinians, perhaps a permanently insurmountable one. Had the United States forced Israel to resettle several thousand Palestinian refugees from the Gaza Strip in the West Bank, the Palestinian problem would be immeasurably less acute today. But Israel wanted to keep the West Bank open for Jewish settlement. About a quarter million Israelis now live in East Jerusalem and the West Bank. The United States ostensibly opposed the settlement enterprise, but in practice it turned a blind eye, all in the spirit of "support for Israel."

As admirers of America, most Israelis enthusiastically followed the election of Barack Obama. They assume that like every American President, Obama will be pro-Israel. On Israel's Independence Day, its citizens will continue to demonstrate patriotism not only to Israel but to America. At major intersections, children hawk plastic flags for drivers to attach to their windows. Some of them are U.S. flags, in addition to Israeli ones. Ten years after their first appearance, however, they are not exactly the same flags. Now they are imported from China.

Returning from Exile
Gianni Riotta

My Dad's life was etched when the Americans liberated Sicily in 1943. He should have been way up North, in Leghorn, at the Naval Academy, his starched white uniform impeccably pressed. But he got sick and returned home on a short leave.

While his friends and fellow cadets went to their deaths, buried at sea in their submarines, he had to find a job and save his family from starvation in a desolate, bombed-out Palermo.

With the Sicilian capital in their hands, the Allies had liberated the most powerful European radio station south of Naples. The famed U.S. Psychological Warfare Branch (PWB) would use the station to broadcast news to frantic listeners in Nazi-occupied Italy. They would entertain the crowds in Sicily with the first radio soap operas, *Romantic Lives of the Great Musicians*: Tonight, "Mozart! How Amadeus composed, How he loved!" Radio Palermo also had a more discreet task: it broadcast coded messages for the newly formed Partisan groups in northern Italy.

Russian-born Sergeant Misha Kamenetzki was the boss. Educated in Rome, he was forced to leave Italy and move to New York with his Jewish family after Mussolini's racial laws in 1938. Kamenetzki fired with gusto all the Fascist reporters and hired new people, including—an anthropological bombshell in 1943 Sicily!—young, brilliant women. A cousin—everything in Palermo, back then and now, starts with a street-smart cousin telling you all about it—told my dad, "Totò, gli Americani are looking for announcers with an impeccable pronunciation to read the war bulletins. You were trained as an actor at the college theater, right? Go try your luck."

Dad went to the station because he needed money for food. Kamenetzki asked a few questions: the Navy had an anti-Fascist aura about it and our cousin was a Socialist—a good thing to be if you were fighting a war against Mussolini. My dad was hired and did his share on the right side of the Good War, reading secret messages for the Partisans: "Giovanni ha i baffi lunghi. . . . Le ciliegie sono mature." ("John has long whiskers. . . . The cherries are ripe.") There's a black-and-white picture that shows him smiling in front of a giant mike: *Listen world, listen to us!* He soon found out that the reporters were making better money than the announcers were. Even more tantalizing, they had access to the crucial K rations, the food that kept the U.S. Army in fighting form; one ration, with its little tins of meat, cheese, and fruit, was enough to keep an entire family from starvation. The Italians' rations were meager—a loaf of stale bread—while the black market, the dreaded Borsa Nera, was controlled by the Mafia. So Totò Riotta took a chance, went to the Sarge, and pleaded, "Could I be a reporter?"

"You got any experience?" Misha asked.

"We had a magazine in college; I contributed a couple of theater reviews."

"Good man. I'll train you for a week. In the meantime you'll get a reporter's paycheck." And the K rations, of course. That night Dad, Mom, my Grandma Adele, and Aunt Sara, along with a rowdy phalanx of starving cousins, had the first party since the war broke out in 1940, free at last to be happy. Dad borrowed a recording of Glenn Miller's *In the Mood* from the station and played it on my Mom's gramophone. (She wasn't my Mom, then, of course, but his sweet-sixteen girlfriend.) The old garden in via Marco Polo 31, fragrant with the tropical plants my great-grandfather Tommaso had smuggled from the Caribbean a generation before, detonated with the sexy, opening saxophone section, followed by Tex Beneke and Al Klink's competing trumpet and trombone. The windows all around the garden popped open, someone brought some wine, and the party roared till dawn. The war was finally over.

Later, Dad liked to reminisce about Kamenetzi's training sessions. The Sarge would casually put his feet up on the imposing walnut desk, pilfered from some deserted Casa del Fascio, the fascists' barracks. A colonel would sometimes rush into the studio barking orders. My dad would stiffen in an awkward salute, but the Sarge didn't flinch. "I am in charge around here," he would remind the colonel.

Totò would remain impressed all his life. "The American Army was casual and relaxed, khaki pants barely pressed. Mussolini had forced even the kids and the housewives into a totalitarian system, making them march in formations every Saturday. The Americans were winning the war but their army was a civilian army, more a fighting summer camp than a killing machine."

Totò's democratic education had just begun. He glued together his first news program, working the wires with scissors and pencil. "It was a tough job," Dad would remember. "North of Naples, people would be hanged if caught by the Gestapo listening to Radio Palermo. You've got to give a great show to such a brave audience. So imagine my surprise when I hand the first bulletin to Kamenetzki, he reads it thoroughly and shoots back, 'Does not work, Totò. It's too good for us. You need something negative for the Allies to close the broadcast. Go back to the wires, find an operation that went FUBAR [military jargon for Fucked Up Beyond All Recognition], you know what that means, right? Keep an eye out for a ship we lost, a town where we are retreating, a couple of downed planes. Italians are fed up with the Duce pro-paganda: Victory forever! If you keep saying all is well, the sun shines all the time, they won't believe you. Totò, believe me: truth is the best propaganda.'"

Misha Kamenetzki passed away in 1995. Some years before, he had changed his name to Ugo Stille in remembrance of a friend killed by the Nazis and later became the editor of *Corriere della Sera*, Italy's best daily newspaper. He hired my dad in 1943 and me in 1987. Same casual style, same attitude: when asked by one of his reporters, "Direttore, what is our position on the Socialist Party congress?" Misha replied simply, "We give all the news."

It was impossible not to love the Americans in my Dad's stories. They all had the elegance of Gregory Peck, the decency of Spencer Tracy, and the dedication of a character in a Frank Capra movie. They seemed always to treasure the truth. We later became radical students and marched in Palermo's old baroque quarters demanding peace in Vietnam, yet we remained staunchly pro-American. We sang "We Shall Overcome" and protested when our brothers were shot at Kent State. Dylan was our soundtrack, Robert Jordan our moral model, Paul Goodman the only writer who really knew how we felt, growing up absurd. In our confused desire for change, we idealized Malcolm X's strength, Reverend King's compassion, and Bobby Kennedy's moral courage.

In school, the exiled Greek students would tell us how Washington was supporting the military junta in their country, the very cradle of democracy. Robert Jordan died fighting against Franco in Hemingway's master-piece, yet the geopolitical strategy of the Cold War made President Eisenhower forget about the past. Franco's iso-lation ended in 1953, when Spain and the United States cosigned the Pact of Madrid, which provided Spain with badly needed loans in return for American military bases. Farewell *Inglés*, adios Robert Jordan. Yet, it didn't mat-ter to us. In Prague a playwright named Vaclav Havel survived Stalinism on a diet of beat poetry, rock 'n' roll, and Lennon; we survived conformism and the dreaded one-dimensional world deprecated by Herbert Marcuse by reciting Arlo Guthrie's lullaby, *You can get anything you want at Alice's restaurant*, the way a Tibetan monk would hum his prayers.

America now sponsored dictatorships all over the world. The historian John Lewis Gaddis talks of the Cold War as the Long Peace, and peace it was for us, in Europe. The adjective *cold* had traditionally overwhelmed the substantive *war*—for us, the war of ideas, emotions, identities, cultures. Washington was often hypocritical, denouncing the T. rex in the Kremlin while feeding its own T. rex in Latin America or Asia. The antidote to nihilism, the sense of loss that eventually drove so many in my generation into the arms of the radical Red Brigade, came from America. Not from the center of power this time, but from the fringe: "I saw the best minds of my generation destroyed by madness." America was the madness, America was the reason.

I was thus educated in the ways of contradiction, a brutal training that allowed me to survive one of the toughest jobs around in the early twenty-first century: being a pro-American writer in Europe. When my friend Charles Kupchan, trying to jumpstart a seminar in Germany right after 9/11, asked his PhD students: "OK, do any of you think we Americans deserved the attack at the World Trade Center?" he expected maybe one person would put a hand up. All the Teutonic hands in the room went up. In Naples, right before the Iraq war, three students cornered me in a dark alley: "So you are Riotta, il filoamericano." Middle age had not mellowed my Sicilian fuck-you attitude. "I am not pro-American, I actually *am* an American. So the fuck what?"

I was indeed an American. After many years working in New York and two American kids I had sworn
allegiance to my new country in the gloomy Federal
Building in downtown Manhattan. It was July 2001, the
Twin Towers still gleaming in the sky. Time was running
out for them; the Fates were ready to cut the threads of
thousands of their tenants' lives. *How they see us, why they
hate us*: the classic American angst was, and is, my angst,
too. On his college application, my son Michele dwelled
on dual identity: "while in Europe," he wrote, "I feel
like an American Ambassador; when at home I spend my
time trying to explain the rest of the world to my friends."
Tough job, Michelino. President Bush's UN Ambassador
John Bolton, during a posh seminar in Venice, so deeply
offended the mostly sympathetic audience that an elderly,
dignified European diplomat started to cry. Misha's
motto was reversed: propaganda had become the only
available truth. At a lunch on beautiful Lago Maggiore
featuring some of the savviest European entrepreneurs,
a brash young neocon speaker lectured on the virtues
of the market to hedge-funders who would make more
money before dessert than the zealous speaker would
before Christmas. America was not listening anymore.
Dad used to praise a nation able to listen to its enemies.
Now the giant seemed deaf even to the voices of friends.

I did not give up. I went to Iraq to cover the war and
wrote about the bombing of the UN building, the killing
of Ambassador Sergio Vieira De Mello, and thwarting of
the UN; I testified before the House of Representatives
on June 17, 2003, about the deterioration of relations
between America and its European allies ("The Future

of Transatlantic Relations: A View from Europe"). I was intimidated and nervous. It was the grotesquely dark hour of Freedom Fries. A ridiculous cafeteria-style food fight raged between Washington and Brussels, pretending to be a trans-Atlantic debate. It was gloomy, it was idiotic, and it was dangerous. I felt like my son, always abroad at home, exiled in the old country, estranged in my new country. When it was my turn to speak, in the imposing ebony-paneled room, I tried yet again to bridge the ocean, reading my lines to the skeptical congressmen:

The recent animosity between Europe and the United States is not rooted in a different set of values. Americans are not from Mars, and Europeans are not from Venus (a Goddess, I must say, to be treated with full respect: after a close reading of Greek mythology, her warlike record is not bad at all and includes the foundation of mighty Rome through her champion Aeneas). Since 1945, Europeans have fought in Vietnam, the Suez, Algeria, Cyprus; the Greeks fought against Turkey; the Portuguese were in Angola, the Brits in the Falklands. And if you think of the Balkans, you'll note that those presumed peaceful Europeans countries were busy waging war at the first opportunity. War was banned only from the continental territories of the founding members of the European Community, thanks to the American nuclear umbrella and the wisdom of leaders. I am thinking of presidents Roosevelt, Truman, Eisenhower, and Kennedy in America and Churchill, Adenauer, De Gasperi, Schumann, and

Monnet in Europe.

Contrary to what many op-ed articles suggest, Europe and the United States do share a code of values. What divides them is a matter of interests. There indeed is a clash of civilization but is not between *us* and *them*, as professor Samuel Huntington suggests. It is the fight between the forces of tolerance and the legions of intolerance, a battle that divides America, the EU, the Third World, all the established religions, academies, and the world of ideas. Many passing interests can divide Europe and America. But if we fail to see that in this small planet the forces of democracy cannot fail to join hands and stand together, that loss of vision, more than any statistics about GNP, inflation, growth, will put in danger the future of our children.

I had ruminated over those lines since September 11, 2001. I had left Manhattan late on September 10, 2001, on a business trip after taking my daughter Anita to her first day of kindergarten. I watched the planes crash on TV and reacted as a father and an editor, intertwining the two identities to make the tightrope I was walking on a little steadier. Through Canada on a chartered plane to Montreal, and then a harrowing long drive home to Manhattan, as desolate as the Palermo of my father's war stories. For a long time, I felt the guilt of not having been in my hometown at its darkest hour. The sweet guy chatting with me at the school bus stop on September

10, while my daughter and his daughter clutched hands, died on 9/11. Where was I?

Yet little by little, after the war in Afghanistan, after my night with the Rangers patrolling blacked-out Sadr City in Baghdad, after the 2004 presidential campaign when yet again a frank debate was obstructed by the elaborate lies of the Swift Boat videos, I began to think it had been a good thing I wasn't in New York when history struck. The rage that I felt after the devastation at the World Trade Center and the Pentagon had obliterated Dad and Misha's lesson. I was in too much pain to listen to any distant voice, friend or foe. Whoever was not part of my pain was a stranger, an enemy. I still respond with fury when some deluded fanatic says to me that America "deserved 9/11." Yet I now see that isolation and hubris generate distrust, and arrogance breeds ignorance.

I often think of Bobby Kennedy's favorite quote from Aeschylus: (*Agamemnon* 179–183):

> *Drop, drop—in our sleep, upon the heart*
> *sorrow falls, memory's pain,*
> *and to us, though against our very will,*
> *even in our own despite,*
> *comes wisdom,*
> *by the awful grace of God.*

In the days following his brother Jack's assassination, Bobby Kennedy found the quote in a wonderful and long-forgotten book, *The Greek Way*, by the great classicist Edith Hamilton. He quoted the verses forty years ago, the day after Martin Luther King's assassination, reciting the passage by heart (and misquoting "despite" as "despair"). Aeschylus was a veteran of the strategic battle of Marathon and fought the way Greeks used to fight, side by side with his brother Cynegeirus. He knew what the culture wars were before they had a name.

But it was after 9/11; no one was listening, each side blinded by its own propaganda. *Le Monde Diplomatique* described America as the new evil empire, while in America the rabid talk-show hosts described Europe as the Axis of Weasels. Hate had won; the Atlantic had become a toxic pond.

Then the 2008 presidential campaign started. In the United States the fight was about Obama and Hillary, and could McCain eventually lure in the conservative voters? In Europe, the bluest of the blue Democratic states, it was a different campaign. Europeans loved Obama for putting it neatly: "Why invade Iraq and not North Korea or Burma? Why intervene in Bosnia and not Darfur? Are our goals in Iran regime change, the dismantling of Iranian nuclear capability, the prevention of nuclear proliferation, or all three? Our allies—and for that matter our enemies—certainly don't know what those answers are. More important, neither do the American people."

Of course there was a lot of romantic infatuation with the energy of Obama. But it was the worldly and skeptical magazine the *Economist*, not one of the boosterish newsweeklies, that splashed its cover with photographs of the two candidates, Obama and McCain, under the headline "America at Its Best." A war hero who sponsored reconciliation with Vietnam against a black American who still had relatives living in African villages. What movie are we watching, a Frank Capra sequel in 2008? This was my Dad's lesson—"there is not a single problem in the world that can be solved without America, but America alone cannot solve any problem"—transformed into a global debate.

America was back. My exile was over.

Marilyn Monroe's Panties

Carmen Boullosa

On the very same day that the astronaut John Glenn orbited the Earth three times, Marilyn Monroe boasted that she, too, had done something quite intrepid: she had traveled to Mexico.

Those are not empty words. Mexico and the United States may be next-door neighbors, but we are nonetheless far apart in spirit. Despite the fact that we share the busiest border crossing in the world, that twenty million of my fellow citizens live in the USA, that our economies are inextricably linked, that we have simply no way of escaping each other, we remain radically different. Both sides have a hard time understanding and knowing who, exactly, lives next door. Really, we are rather like those classic marriages of yesteryear, a couple irreversibly bound by fate and family, with no possibility of divorce. We have totally irreconcilable personalities; we seethe with mutual scorn, yet we sleep side by side, in separate beds. Between us the Rio Grande, a river whose waters alternately flow and dry at various spots along its course.

When Marilyn Monroe made her now-famous trip to Mexico, the first thing she did was request an audience with the First Lady, who had championed the cause of serving free breakfasts in the country's public schools. When the two women met, Marilyn handed the First Lady a donation, a check in the amount of two thousand U.S. dollars, "for the children of Mexico." President López Mateos, who in the middle of the Cold War described himself as a "pragmatic leftist" and was reputed to be something of a Don Juan, received the actress behind closed doors in the Presidential Palace. Under the genteel protection of a Mexican ambassador, she was squired from the city center to Xochimilco, where she admired the canals, the flower-festooned *chalupa* boats, the music (mariachi and otherwise), the quesadillas served, freshly made, from the canoes. . . .

The newspapers dedicated page after page to Marilyn, who then traveled to Taxco, the beautiful colonial mining town in the state of Guerrero where *La Bandida* was being filmed. The movie featured the illustrious Emilio (El Indio) Fernández acting alongside *La Doña, La Mexicana*—María Félix, the paradigm of Mexican beauty and one of the legendary divas of our domestic cinema. Upon learning of Monroe's visit, Félix refused to meet the "gringa."

I was seven years old when la Monroe came to our country, and in my house nary a word was mentioned about her junket. Nothing was said about the lover she supposedly took upon arrival, a producer by the name of Bolaños with whom she traveled to Acapulco, and then to Los Angeles, where the affair ended. Nor did I hear a word about the parties, cocktail gatherings, or restaurants she graced with her presence in the company of Cantinflas and other Mexican luminaries. All I heard was that Marilyn Monroe was a "gringa," nothing more specific than that. Not a single mention of how, in the legendary Continental Hotel in the city center, a photographer immortalized her crossing her impossibly white legs and revealing that she wore absolutely nothing beneath her dress. Nor did anyone in my house talk of the crowds that gathered outside her hotel chanting her name, or of the generous check she gave to help the poor. Nothing. "Gringa." To call it pejorative is an understatement that barely describes the weight of a term uttered by women perched atop the high horse of Mexican aristocracy. "From the remote past / upon the great pyramids of Teotihuacán / upon the teocallis and the volcanoes / upon the bones and the crosses of the golden conquistadors / time grows in silence," goes the poem "Del pasado remoto" by the renowned Salvador Novo, in his day the chronicler of Mexico City.

The women who sat around our family dinner table called her "gringa" not because she was a divorcée—in my house divorcées were not mentioned because mine was a traditional family that, for a time, had had a brief flirtation with Opus Dei. No, they despised her because she was a "gringa," a woman who wore no panties. They despised her because they themselves thought they were so elegant. The women in my family knew they had style, plenty of it—after all, they were citizens of a country with thirty centuries of history behind it. Up there to the north of the Río Bravo (as we call it), the gringos were a bunch of upstart cowboys, brutes that possessed neither culture nor tradition.

(But there is something else that strikes me about Marilyn Monroe's missing panties. Imbedded in the Mexican collective consciousness is the belief that indigenous women do not use underclothes beneath their traditional dress. And looking back now, I can't help but wonder if there wasn't a hint of denigration in that nasty remark, a reprise of the Malinche myth, the myth of the raped woman, whose legs are always open "for the master" in what is a particular variant of slavery. For Malinche had given Cortés the key to conquer our country. It had to be in Mexico, Marilyn, where they took that photograph of you without your panties on. Only in Mexico, where the indigenous women, as the legend goes, don't wear panties, either.)

Getting back to what was said and not said in my house, one thing I do remember quite well is lengthy descriptions of the astronaut John Glenn's great feats. During after-dinner conversations, his exploits were enumerated in lavish detail, though I must say that my family failed to mention that he, like Marilyn, was also a "gringo." Surely, this omission was due to the fact that Glenn was different—unlike Marilyn, his conquests were "for mankind."

The same year that Marilyn toured Mexico, our country welcomed other visitors from the north, such as the Kennedys, who also caused a sensation. Thousands upon thousands gathered at the airport, and even more lined the road that carried them, in a convertible, to the National Palace, and still more venerated the couple when they went to mass at the Basilica of the Virgin of Guadalupe. Yet, part of what made the Kennedys such a dazzling success in Mexico, and all across Latin America for that matter, was the fact that they were gringos, but then again, they weren't—not really. At the end of the day, JFK's family was Irish Catholic, and Jacqueline was not only not blonde but she actually spoke Spanish, which meant that she was an "educated" person, not just another "dumb gringa." So they weren't totally gringos—not real gringo gringos in the truest sense, at least. They wore underwear beneath their formal clothes, they attended mass, and they ate real meals at the middle of the day, not the typical American "lonch," as we called it.

Lonch: in the movie *Primero soy mexicano* (*First I Am a Mexican*), Joaquín Pardavé (a *zarzuela* singer and actor with a special gift for comedy) plays a man living in Mexico whose son, now living in the USA, comes to pay him a visit. Here, the point is driven home quite clearly: in this movie, the nutritional mores of our neighbors to the north are considered the stuff of wild beasts. "*Lonch?*" the father asks his son. "What kind of insanity, what kind of atrocity is that? We are cultivated people, we eat a *comida*, not '*lonch*.'"

The so-called American Way of Life is the butt of many a joke, as well, in the comedy by Juan Bustillo de Oro, *Acá las tortas* (*Here, Tortas*) [n.b.: tortas are a kind of sandwich that Mexicans find totally different from the sandwiches served across the border], a film that revisits the topic of those nutcases up north. At the family dinner table, the adults wile away the hours in conversation, eating not *lonch* but many of the delicacies of the exquisite cuisine of Tabasco—turtle soup, shark bread, layers of tortillas, shark cooked in tomato sauce, and fried black beans, stuffed hens, Basque-style codfish, lizard-fish tamales, stuffed Dutch cheese, *copa nevada*—a kind of *île flotant*—burnt milk.

My father worked his entire life at a "proud to be Mexican" company that made (very white) industrial bread—sliced bread—that was far from a local tradition, having been imported thanks to "gringo" technology. He had studied chemistry at the Jesuit university because his family believed that was the profession of the future, a popular notion in those days; my mother went to the same university to study chemistry as well, and that is how and where they met. Later on in Minnesota, after he was married but before he graduated, my father took a course in bread production that ultimately produced the topic for the thesis that earned him his degree, and he told me that in the Twin Cities he and my mother would go to baseball games. I can only assume they also must have eaten those classic American *lonches* as well. Looking back on my father's profession, another Salvador Novo quote comes to mind: "Night: Worker, I don't mean to say I am a socialist / but you have spent the entire day / taking care of machines invented by Americans / to take care of needs invented by Americans."

At home it was never suggested that my father's work had anything at all to do with the Americans—his company was one hundred percent Mexican—nor were the words *worker* or *socialists* ever uttered. "Christianity yes,

Communism no" stickers were fundamental elements of my family life back then. Yet my father could not hide the fury and desolation he felt when the La Azteca chocolate company was sold to "the gringos." I remember it well; we were in the car when he started complaining: "Now, every time a Mexican child eats a Carlos Quinto [a favorite sweet treat in those days] the gringos will get even richer. Wasn't Almonris enough?" he fumed, referring to another childhood candy, produced by Chocolates Larín, which had already been taken over by "the gringos." Every time another Mexican company "fell into the clutches of the gringos," it was a day of mourning for us—those cowboys from the north were so greedy. My father's horror reached its peak when a U.S. company began to compete with his in the production and sale of sliced bread; I remember hearing him say how this could be the end of everything, that the gringos knew all there was to know—marketing ploys, sneaky tactics, bribing unions, and government officials. They were utterly without scruples, and they came armed with all of Uncle Sam's money and might. I heard the main points of this lecture one Sunday morning as my father contemplated the full-page advertisement that Sunbeam bread had taken out in *El Excelsior*, "the newspaper of our nation's life." Oh, it was impossible to compete with the gringos. Luckily there were laws that protected us, laws that declared "Mexico for the Mexicans."

Nationalist sentiment—that is, Mexico for the Mexicans—was not limited to September 15, our Independence Day, when the entire populace explodes in a countrywide celebration of epic proportions. Mexico was ours. The gringos had already robbed us of Texas and made off with another sizable chunk of our territory, but we had reclaimed our oil. Our iciest disdain was reserved for the *prestanombres*, the name-lenders: mercenary lawyers who would sell their names to the gringos who wanted to purchase properties that by law were off-limits to Americans.

As we Mexicans reveled in our gringophobia, we also indulged in our own brand of domestic racism: against the Indians. Of course, the Indians that were our nation's ancestors were brilliant, sublime, but those that lived among us in the here-and-now were relegated to the most abject poverty, expelled from our contemporary worldview, all within the conviction that Mexico is a *mestizo* country.

(To go back to Marilyn's panties for a moment: in the prudish Mexico of those days, anyone who gazed at that photo that disrobed her so publicly was, in effect, penetrating the gringa, for the image had the effect of giving her up to the people.)

As for the industrial bread that rested in the hands of our family's professional expert, my father explained, in a way that almost sounded like a justification, that his company made their sliced bread because it traveled better, stayed fresher longer, didn't get soggy or hard at the drop of a hat. But most important, he said, they made the bread because they were able to do so under the most hygienic conditions—it was sanitary, healthy. And when he said those words I had no idea that they were in fact very gringo-esque criteria. Which reminds me once again of a poem by Salvador Novo, this time his "Frida Kahlo": "the cereals full of vitamins the spinach full of time." Now, ever since my earliest childhood I knew of nothing more exquisite than a *bolillo*, our white bread, or a corn tortilla, neither of which was produced in very hygienic conditions, according to my father—the bakers who churned out *bolillos* would wipe the sweat from their brows with the dough they kneaded. Nor did their products stay fresh for more than a day, and they traveled quite miserably.

At the time when Marilyn Monroe came to Mexico, I still had not begun to play with Barbies, nor eat Sweetarts or Hershey's Kisses—once I did, they were pure paradise for me, stiff competition for the Carlos Quinto candies, the *almonris* chocolates, the Cerezo marzipans, and the nonindustrial, hand-prepared green mangos on a stick with piquín chilies that I have since seen for sale on street corners in New York (that's Mexican export technology for you!), the tamarind balls, the almond squares, and the homemade chocolate bars that my grandmother made in her kitchen. I got my hands on Kisses and Barbies only because my father brought them back directly from the land up north; they were not for sale in Mexico—the market was protected. Our country was very stingy when it came to granting import licenses for all kinds of products, and it was expressly forbidden to import things like household appliances and other such goods.

My father occasionally traveled to Gringoland for professional reasons. To manufacture sliced bread, one had to stay on top of innovations in the industry. But he was happy to return home. "Poor gringos!" I always thought, with the aristocratic prejudice of those who come from a culture thirty centuries old, as I connected the dots between the many things I had heard here and there about life in America: "They live in deserted wastelands they call 'suburbia,'" I said to myself, "in a country that isn't anywhere near as beautiful [or certainly not as cute] as ours." That was because the gringos didn't have San Luis Potosí, or the lovely city of Zacatecas, or Guanajuato, or Mexico City—which, unlike the nightmare it is today, was a beautiful city back then, with roundabouts and fountains, lush promenades blooming with dahlias, trams that traversed the city with ease, and volcanoes that loomed over us from the edges of our tall valley. Nor did the gringos have beaches nearly as breathtaking as ours, obviously—otherwise, what were all those "gringas" doing in Acapulco, making fools of themselves as they kissed the *lancheros* who drove the tourist boats? Precisely because we possessed such great wealth and they possessed nothing but a barren, almost suffocating wilderness, we had to protect ourselves from them—how could we help but feel afraid that they might want to make off with all that belonged to us?

And so, when la Monroe paid her visit to Mexico, the weight of that word, *gringo*, was crystal clear to me, despite the fact that I was only seven at the time. *Gringo* was a word that implied scorn, that saw the American Way of Life as the domain of rude, vulgar heathens. But as soon as I abandoned my Barbies and other childhood whims—this was before the computer age—it did not take long for me to become a fan of Bob Dylan and the Rolling Stones, to get kissed for the first time to the strains of Muddy Waters, and to declare Martin Luther King Jr. my all-time hero. Not long after that, I chanced upon my very first copy of *Ms.* magazine, started wearing embroidered blouses from Oaxaca, worshipped Cortázar and Neruda, and thought to myself, with all the force I could muster: "Yankee go home!" In this I was actually joined by some gringo friends, the kind that Salvador Novo describes in the previously cited poem "Del pasado remoto," almost putting his words in the mouth of my mother, grandmother, and aunts: "yanqui / defeated by the machine that engendered his comforts / bewildered, driven mad by the noises of industry, / missionary, tourist, journalist, / great blond thinkers who arrived in an airplane. / Another man said: 'With a few Ford tractors, / a few Crane toilets, / a few kilometers of paved roads / Mexico will be the paradise / that the United States failed to become.'"

In the 1980s, with Salinas de Gortari and the NAFTA accord, things took a turn, though not 180 degrees. The "gringo" no longer needed those name-lenders to buy and possess. Imports entered the country unrestricted. Small companies went bankrupt. Immigration to the United States—illegal, of course, just like those Barbies, Sweetarts, and record players of my childhood—rose dramatically. And "our" banks suddenly became gringo banks.

But now, so many years later, in the age of computers and iPods, one thing that has not changed is that love-hate feeling about the United States. Or, to borrow the words of the Familia Burrón, protagonists of one of Mexico's most widely read comic books, the USA is "the land of the blonds . . . *los estates*" (our way of saying "the States"). The Familia Burrón is the apotheosis of urban Mexican existence, living in a *vecindad,* a kind of crumbling palace where families gather around a central courtyard, creating something of a community infrastructure as they wash their clothes and occasionally cook meals together, talking in their neighborhood slang and believing family and solidarity to be life's most prized possessions. The cover of the October 16, 2001, edition of the comic book features Gamucita, a ninety-year-old woman, dragging her broken-down, tattered suitcase held shut by two pieces of string, the soles of her shoes pockmarked with holes, alongside an arrow pointing toward the United States. She makes the journey on foot because she cannot afford to travel any other way. She has no choice but to abandon her home because she makes her living by washing and ironing other people's clothes, and now the water has run out. She and her son are hungry. What follows is the dialogue between them and the Burrón family, the protagonists of this comic book series: "My little mother and I had a serious argument because I swore to her that I would go anywhere—anywhere except the land of those blond people. . . . " "But your mother knows you'll find work there." "I don't doubt it, but that's where all the bad Mexicans go, dragging our reputation through the mud, putting their miserable lives on display. No, I can't . . . the day I go to *los estates* will be when I get invited to give lectures at the great gringo universities. To go there because we're broke, forget it—I'd rather die than set foot on the other side." "Good-for-nothing!" "Instead of going over there to bust your ass picking cotton or sweeping streets, you let your mother go instead so that she can cough up a lung from working so hard?" "I don't have an ass—I'm an intellectual."

There are a number of interesting things to be gleaned from this little scenario: firstly, the idea that it is possible for even a ninety-year-old woman to reach the USA by foot. That this is her only chance to escape poverty. That émigrés are always the weakest, the neediest of us all.

Twenty million Mexicans live and work in the United States, the ones who bust their asses as well as the "lazy" intellectuals (like Gamucita's son). Mexico's number one source of money transfers comes from its émigrés, whose deposits now exceed those generated by the country's oil income—all of which makes me wonder if, in the age of globalization, our exported folk continue to feel what Piporro felt in the movie *El Pocho*. Rejected by his own countrymen, yet despised by the gringos because he "is neither from here nor there," he just stays in between, floating in the waters of the Río Bravo.

Our ambivalence toward the United States could not be more patent: on one hand antigringo sentiment is stronger than ever in Mexico, but gringo sympathies have not weakened, either. The people have changed: now we have Britney Spears and Paris Hilton, Bush and the war in Iraq, and Obama. Times change. But memories and prejudices have a way of staying the same.

Dear America
Abdelkader Benali

Of all historical mistakes, you are the most exceptional one and you know it. It is for that reason that the immigrant, the historical mistake par excellence, is attracted to put down roots in you, because lots of historical accidents—all those brilliant blunders—make one great glowing gem.

I also see my writing career as a historical mistake. The only way to deal with this mistake is by embracing it and making the most of it. To live the contradiction, as it were. Illiterate parents from the Moroccan Rif settled in Rotterdam, Netherlands, with hopes of a better life and good schooling for their children, and, in time, a video-recorder. One kid becomes a writer. Such bad luck!

My writing career started with a writing competition run by a Dutch newspaper that won me a trip to one of your greatest jewels, New York—the platinum tooth in your already richly filled mouth. As you can see, we were doomed to be together. Had the prize been a trip to Stockholm I would not have tried nearly as hard.

When I first set foot on American soil, I was eighteen or so, an age at which you are erotically susceptible to everything, from Italian football to Mahler's Fifth. It was my first trip across the ocean. Michael Jordan, Richard Pryor, and Michael J. Fox didn't mean anything yet. I tried out my Yankee English on the black taxi driver and my poetry on the skyline. I stammered out sentences in which words like *shining*, *sharp*, *majestic*, and, yes, even *unreachable*, lit up like glittering diamonds. I was set up in a hotel not far from Madison Square Garden. I claimed to hear the balls falling through the basketball nets. At that time I knew the stats of all the Chicago Bulls players by heart. In the hotel lobby stood a cowboy. Nothing was far away, everything was within reach.

Pocketing my first dollars, this Moroccan-European gypsy with his tent, bear, tambourine, and tricks up his sleeve to win the public's charm, began a personal odyssey through this city. I was forced to redefine my lazy definitions of space, time, and mass. Einstein needed a train journey from Basel to B; you became my Basel where I saw that time is elasticity molded in concrete. On the street I heard Arabic being spoken, into which I read that this city, like old Babylon, attracts astrologers, and where there is astrology there are opportunities. My family and I made our way to the Apollo Theater, where the soul's independence was confirmed again. That evening I went to bed with a 104-degree, culture-induced fever.

You were then being led by Clinton, a president who—with all his hyperintelligent charm, with that round face that could laugh so openly and shamelessly at Yeltsin's bumbling, with the tone in which he shared his bedroom secrets with the world—already felt dated, worn-out, a mistake that needed to make way for other mistakes.

*

Everything I ate in New York was fried and sticky. In a stand-up comedy café I drank Coca-Cola out of a glass bucket and to celebrate my crossing I stole the bucket, took it with me to my hotel, and wrapped it in newspaper to take back to Europe.

The high point of the trip at that point? The World Trade Center. It seemed as if the whole visit was built around this small pilgrimage. So many floors that we passed at flying speed to reach the top where we could look out over all that teeming history. Here I am, I thought, standing in the keyhole, the Borgesian Aleph of all historical mistakes. The front portal to everything. Here is where the key is turned with surprising, unexpected, and often destructive consequences for all. Helicopters and propeller-planes came by. What, I wondered, if a little plane flew through this keyhole into the past, present, and future, what would that little place open, what smell would come through the opened door?

Content with this thought I floated back down again. The World Trade Center gained as *lieu de memoire*. Nothing could temper my enthusiasm—the immigrant's antidote to a hostile world—not even my worn-out shoes. In my hotel room I pierced a blister. The moisture that flowed over my foot was this church's holy water.

Whoever, like you, has given oneself the task of being exceptional in all things, must find it hard to bear when you see it copied, stolen, and perfected by others. They've taken your greatest treasure from you. Others seem to be able to do it just as well—better, quicker, and with less fuss. Their steep growth curves recall the nineteenth cen-

tury. The Wild West in the East and *you* can't go back to
the beginning to rise again like a phoenix from the ashes
and start the struggle anew. You've built up an impres-
sive list of achievements. History is on your side. But now
what? The privileges you awarded yourself in exchange
for the generosity with which you handed out the fruits
of your labor and talent border on the monstrous—even
that behavior has been copied. The only thing they can't
take away from you is your manhood. They can squeeze
your balls from time to time to see what happens. To see
if you are still a man or have since taken on effeminate
ways *a la* Rome in decline. Sitting back and enjoying the
status you have achieved is not in your nature. You need
to win, to destroy. During those days America showed
me that when one is exceptional—in contrast to Dutch
morality—nothing is absurd.

My stay in New York was not yet over. The day before
my departure to stable, washed-out, gray Europe, I felt a
rejection of my roots, my family, and the Netherlands. I
thought everything should resemble America. I wanted
to live the future and decided that the only way to make
this happen was to stay in New York and, like the Arabs
I'd seen days before in the street, become the astrologer
of my own destiny. I'm a Sagittarius and my mother pre-
dicted I would try to grab it all. My parents didn't want
me being taken for a ride. They had come along because
they thought I was too young for tourist solitude. I was
going to show them that wasn't the case.

I needed to go into hiding and decided to move

into an enormous bookshop where I had bought Ralph Ellison's *Invisible Man* the day before.

When my parents realized my disappearance, they would notify the police and file a missing person's report. But ultimately they would decide there was no point to staying in the city and return home. I know the Dutch; once they've satisfied their emotional and administrative duty, they sail off.

At 10:00, I packed my bags and walked on my thread-bare shoes to the subway. Ten bandages on each foot. I left a note in the hotel for my parents: "Don't look for me." I didn't write it to reassure but as a warning, as evidence of my determination. When I had left the hotel, it occurred to me that writing "leave me alone" would have been better. Was that not what I had always strived for? To finally put an end to the relentless pressure to prove yourself, be known, do your duty laid down by others? New York frees you from the responsibility of not letting anyone down.

To kill the few hours before moving into the bookshop, I visited the Metropolitan Museum of Art. I determined that my first step would be to stride from room to room in search of the artwork that would calm my nerves. The second step was to swap the sticky, fried food for a sand-wich of sorts. Third, I needed to find a job. On the steps of the Metropolitan I wrote the following lines in my notebook: *It has begun. Nothing can stop me. The casts are off. Now just an American girlfriend. Relationships are everything.* In the distance I heard the scream of sirens possibly looking for me or, like the Sirens of Odysseus, trying to tempt me back home.

Not long after I had sat down in a café to begin my autobiography, a beautiful woman came in. *Relationships are everything*. It wasn't difficult to make contact because she sat down next to me and I was eloquent. Within five minutes I had told her about my aspirations. I quoted Theroux, Marlowe, and the Marx Brothers. I hoped I came across as one of the crazy Marx-characters. She listened with interest, left me her card, and told me to contact her if I got stuck. In the Netherlands I had been given the advice to never take up this kind of invitation— it's American politeness, not to be confused with hospitality. I felt she was different.

In the Barnes & Noble I had chosen as temporary accommodation I reclined on a big leather sofa in the fiction department and started taking books off the shelves at random. My enthusiasm boiled over when my eye fell on a small book containing the Declaration of Independence. Though I had company—a dark man was sitting in a corner with his head in an Asian cookbook—I started feeling lonely. I must have radiated this because I was suddenly approached by the same woman I had met in the café. She smiled at me and walked over to the cookbook area.

"Is this the book you are looking for?" I asked her and handed her the Asian cookbook I had removed from under the dark man's nose.

"Yes, this is the book I was looking for. I have a guest this evening who I am cooking for." Things were going in the right direction. I told her about my experience with ginger and black bean sauce (the short-lived relationship I had with the Chinese daughter of a take-away restaurant was bearing fruit). Unfortunately she had to leave and the moment she was gone the loneliness of the adventurer descended upon me again. I tackled my weariness by diving into the books; eating some chocolate cookies and then more chocolate cookies. Slowly my patience began to run out. The shop was closing. Without external stimulus my willpower began to fade. I decided not to spend the night in the bookshop. Standing in front of a cozy, warm restaurant, I worked out what I wanted to eat from the menu, what it would cost me, and then decided not to do it—a quick sum informed me I would have used up my dollars before reaching the main course. It was about getting through the first day, I told myself. Tomorrow everything would be easier. Perhaps it was a good idea to get a job via the back door? The Mexican boy washing up looked at me with glassy eyes, shouted something in an American dialect to someone, and received a response that he summarized as NO! I retorted him with my biggest greeting: *hasta la victoria sempre.* I searched in my bag for the last chocolate cookie and found the card of the woman who had taken the Asian cookbook from me. Close examination of the map showed me she lived just a stone's throw away, a mere forty-five minutes away. She had said I could call her if I was stuck. I reckoned that moment had come. I had a sudden strong desire for Chinese soup.

The taxi driver took me as far as my money allowed. We had an animated conversation about the world we lived in. He from the Punjab, me from the Rif. I asked if he knew of a job for someone who knew how to work hard. We parted as friends.

Her name is Catherine. She comes from the Midwest and is blonde. She doesn't seem surprised. "You really had nowhere left to go," she said with a smile.

"Yes, you are my last refuge."

"Welcome."

I sat on the sofa in her apartment. She vanished, shuffled past, and vanished again. She asked if I wanted a drink. I said anything nonfizzy was fine. I was handed a glass of red wine. When she came back she asked me to follow her to the dining room.

"Weren't you expecting a guest?"

"Yes, he has arrived." The table was set for two. We ate the Asian dishes we had spoken about in the bookshop. I couldn't eat with chopsticks so I used a knife and fork. She asked me endlessly about the Netherlands, I asked her endlessly about New York. She said my eyes shone. I said it was because of her.

The enthusiasm that had characterized you—in Ishmael of *Moby Dick*, Portnoy of *Portnoy's Complaint*, Moses Herzog of *Herzog*, Huckleberry in *Huckleberry Finn*—received a massive blow when the towers fell on September 11. The keyhole vanished out of sight. The key was lost and had to be searched for among the rubble, the dead, and the molten bronze artworks. The key had melted. And we could only look on, partly shocked, partly involved, and largely unsure and nervous about the consequences of your rancor.

And then the bombs began to fall. On Kabul, on Baghdad. Maybe one day in Iran. Like every empire you wipe out that shows your weaknesses. You burn to the ground the painful contradictions brought to light by the gap between saying and doing. In this you are no different from other empires. Only you do it with a smile. With no rush. With an enthusiasm that is contagious. A B-52 is a basketball player who scores basket after basket. Haruki Murakami wrote in his afterword for *The Wind-Up Bird Chronicle* that he was in America at the time of the first Gulf War and he sensed an enthusiasm for the coming war. The idea alone united people, he said, gave them a goal. A self-appointed mission to free the world of the bad guys. We are on that track again. If empires are good for something it is for making war. Nothing exceptional about that, you just know how to, with your charm, make it exceptional in execution and style.

Someone knocked on the door. My supervisors said it was time to go. "In one hour at the reception desk. We're off!" I had the taste of salt in my mouth. Drank water. How did I get from her to here. I remembered that Catherine had gone for a walk with me. She had to be at work early the next day, in five hours time in fact so she couldn't make it a late one. I understood. The Mexican who told me there was no work for me in the restaurant walked by. He didn't recognize me. I took a shower, changed my clothes, and decided not to think about it anymore. The adventure was over. In the taxi back to the airport I was so quiet the supervisor asked if I was ill.

"No," I said, "just a little tired."

*

The only souvenir was the glass I had stolen. That evening I gave it to my father. He looked at it and said, "How beautiful, a flower vase." I said nothing but had to laugh. Europe would never understand America, not even this resident immigrant. But the vase never saw flowers. The next day it slipped out of my hand. Gravity pulled it groundward and it shattered into a thousand giggling tears.

The American Empire: A Libretto in Eight Movements

Chris Abani

1.

The consensus among non-Americans seems to be that we all know how to be better Americans than the Americans. There is of course a disguised envy to this assertion. It implies that we are more compassionate, moral, inclusive, and reflective. The envy I refer to is simply that of wanting the gains of America, but none of the culpability for wielding the privilege these gains bring.

The terms *America* and *American* have come to suggest both a place and an identity. This means that the thinking that marks one as American or a place as America, through global capitalism and the spread of America-driven consumerism, has become available from rural Arkansas to Kenya and Romania and Russia. The ability to think of oneself as a conceptual American is an interesting phenomenon, and it leads outsiders to feel particularly invested in the investigation of the term, partly because of their connection to it, and partly because their own ability to conceptualize themselves is now connected to the identity of America and Americans.

This creates a strange sense of personal betrayal on the part of these non-native Americans when America undermines their idolization of it, because it speaks directly to their own identity. How can one believe uncritically in a religion that betrays its adherents?

By their empire of mythology, a mythology propagated worldwide through popular culture, Americans have made this possible. We noncertified Americans can now legitimately question, not only what it means to be an American, but also what and where is "America." Over coffee in a Starbucks-clone café in Sarajevo, M. raises a new question: where is NOT America?

2.

Perhaps because we speak English (in Nigeria and America), our conversations about place and desire for place, between each other and among ourselves, are always mediated through Europe. I say this because the use of English invokes the specter of the British Empire, a specter whose shadow falls not only over Europe but also its former colonies, including America and Nigeria. It is easier, I think, for America to ignore this specter, but in Nigeria, the balance of power is against us.

In Nigeria, we try to negotiate this difficulty by searching for an identity of defiance, of rejection of Europe and its colonizing erasure of us. It remains confusing to me why in rejecting Europe in general and England in particular, we in Nigeria took so readily to the American dream and its offer of a land of newness and opportunity for all.

In America, on the other hand, the flirtation is with the rejection of Europe as intellectual and perhaps even moral ancestor while simultaneously courting its acceptance. Sadly, as in all Oedipal moments, there is no acceptance from the parent. Europe resoundingly snubs America. There are many complicated reasons for this, I am sure, but I think that at the core it is the fact that the Europeans who didn't get to go to the New World will always resent those who did. Mainly because in much of old world Europe (generalizations are inadequate but functional here), suffering has been elevated to the status of a religion, a fervent worship of inconvenience, a total rejection of any kind of ease, while across the Atlantic, the reverse applies: Americans have become devotees of excess.

I know this because my English mother raised me with an extreme sense of frugality and the perception that Americans are overindulged teenagers, while we Europeans, if you can call a biracial Nigerian "European," exercise control. In more recent times, this sense of an out-of-control adolescent has been behind the various critiques of America as an imperialist nation rampant with power. While I do believe that American imperialism is destructive and its sense of entitlement unbridled, I have grown tired of this European sport of Yankee bashing because I think it is easy and because the Europeans have no moral authority to do so. Not so long ago, they owned much of the rest of the world and treated everyone as their conquest the way Americans now do, with the exception that they never brought us

Starbucks and McDonalds—and as someone said to me on a recent trip to Doha in Qatar, "the great Satan may be forced out of the Middle East, but we are keeping the fast food."

3.

The average Nigerian has an ambivalent relationship to the United States. The terrible truth is that we have come to realize that America is essential, indispensable, and necessary in the careful balance of power in the world. America's power and necessity are not the problem. What is often at the root of its excess and abuses is that America realizes just how essential and powerful it is, and like a tyrannical prom queen, has gone out of control in the exercise of said power.

A Pew Center poll showed that fifty percent of people around the world resent American power: that is a lot of people. Fifty percent of Nigeria alone is somewhere between 75 to 100 million people. I can't distance myself from this resentment, but the term *American power* has been extended to mean "America and Americans," such that the poll has been interpreted as saying that fifty percent of the world resents America and Americans. This calumny reveals (and, ironically, demonstrates) more about the problem of being American—the lack of nuance in approaching issues—than it does about actual public opinion. While the American government's use of power might be resented, the rest of the world doesn't necessarily resent American people, or even the American way of life, regardless of other governments' propaganda (and it is propaganda). I know for a fact that Nigerians—and by extension it would be safe to include many others—are more complex in their understanding of America than Americans are. At the heart of this ambivalence are the good things about America that appeal to people across the globe—choice, leisure, affluence, and freedom—all of which are couched within an attractive informality.

We see this informality expressed in language. The ability of the American language to absorb words and expressions from immigrant cultures and make them its own is an example. This adaptability is made more important when you realize that there has been a strong Turkish presence in Germany for nearly forty years now, and yet no Turkish words have made it into German. The informality with regard to dress and ritual is also often admired. You will never find a Nigerian CEO who comes to meetings in jeans, or a Nigerian president who thinks being ribbed on *Saturday Night Live* is funny. This informality is a thin veneer though, and not a true marker of an egalitarian society. The informality of the language disappears very quickly when there is a need to defend or vilify or rationalize. It eerily switches to bureaucratic jargon—*collateral damage*, *terrorist*, etc.

While the rest of the world holds complex, often contradictory, multifaceted, and ambiguous ideas about America, Americans seem incapable of the type of nuanced self-reflection—they tend to oversimplify. There is a distinction between the American state in these views and Americans and their popular culture (which has become the popular culture of the world).

The United States has become like Israel, where any kind of critique of the apparatus of state becomes couched in racist or fundamentalist terms (hate from outsiders, treason from insiders). But no one feels that way when critiquing, say, China or even Africa. Nobody would argue, least of all Africans themselves, that criticizing Mugabe makes a white person racist. The terms of engagement are different. This suggests a primacy in thinking that makes American lives or American thought superior to the lives and thought of the rest of the world. One only has to look at the recent ads aimed at the Arab world, which show images of happy Muslims in America, geared no doubt to convince the "terrorists" that America is hardly the great Satan if their kin thrive there. This shows a fundamental assumption that the rest of the world is stupid. That the tinsel of Hollywood would fool us when American foreign policy remains unchanged.

4.

Many Americans will argue that they don't have an empire. It is true that because the American empire is mostly an empire of mythology, unlike the old empires of Rome and Britain, it can be hard to pin down, or hold onto, but it exists. America exports this mythology of a benevolent capitalism tinged with freedom via consumerism and only ever exercises its occupationist tendencies when it encounters a society that rejects the mythology of freedom. This new form of empire is pernicious and endemic and also provides the perfect smokescreen preventing reflexivity on the part of Americans. Is there an American who does not at least occasionally believe in a mythical, benevolent vision of the country? This America, while currently lost, is believed to have existed in some recent past. This kind of nostalgia means nothing to a Nigerian who knows the CIA has had a hand in every military coup in the country from 1960 on, not to mention that Americans exterminated Native Americans, enslaved Africans, and put the Japanese in camps.

Newt Gingrich says America is a different kind of empire. He maintains that it has no interest in conquering territories, but only in getting people to believe in their own freedom. What this of course neglects to acknowledge is that Americans do occupy territories that won't allow America's definition of freedom. The freedom Americans want people to accept is the freedom of empire. Noam Chomsky has argued that America was founded as an empire of liberty whose belief has been to spread this liberty over the western hemisphere and beyond. There may be something to that assertion. Sometimes we have to go back to go forward. Most Americans think of the nation as a sanctuary for those who fled oppression elsewhere, and while that is true for many new groups, it didn't apply to the Puritans. The Puritans were forced out of Europe for trying to force everyone else to conform to their ideas of piety and conduct.

5.

Americans speak of freedom, yet squander it each day. In a country where people are actually allowed to think and speak for themselves without direct consequence, they choose to cash it in for easy consumerism.

In my experience, the more educated the non-American,

the more nuanced his analysis, the more complicated and contradictory his approach to the question of America. If education is in fact a factor in this, then one has to wonder why the country with the most educated people seems completely unable to afford itself the same privilege.

Resentment of America's wealth is often more precisely a resentment of the fact that a nation so wealthy will not share with nations whose misfortune is in some way a result of America's acquisition of excess. The reality of the world we live in is that things are unfairly imbalanced in favor of America and Americans, and yet this privilege goes unacknowledged in any way other than platitudes. Don't tell me there isn't enough food to feed everybody. Don't tell me that America doesn't pay its farmers to dump food so that they can control prices. Don't tell me you don't know why the world doesn't like this part of you.

6.

The movies America makes and exports allow Americans to always be the hero, in their mind and in their self-promotion. The American Way is always one of bluster and bloody, explosion-riddled rescues. The decency that all its heroes are allowed is not accorded the foreigners in these films. As Rambo and Chuck Norris tear through the world while saving it, the rest of the world is cast as villain or victim. It is of course *your* film industry, and you can make whatever films you want and export them, but be aware that we are not stupid. When we consume these films, we see the way they reflect, or seem to have influenced, your foreign policy.

I was asked to speak to a group of young school kids in a poor Los Angeles neighborhood about my experiences as an activist in Nigeria, and to show these kids the true privilege they might have should they choose to exercise it. A group of young boys wanted to know why America hadn't sent a battalion of helicopter gunships and marines to kick the shit out of the motherfuckers who were holding me against my will. Damn, one of them added, I would never let anybody hold my boy like that. Not wanting to point out the error of his logic in that a lot of his "boys" were being held right now in penitentiaries across California, I explained instead that the American government didn't know I was imprisoned and if it did would more than likely not have cared. I also asked him about the innocent people who would die in such an extraction should it indeed be allowed to take place. The general consensus in the class, one that even the teacher shared, was that it would have been worth it. In that moment, I realized that regardless of class, race, politics, gender, or any other obvious difference, it seemed that most Americans shared the idea that their lives were more valuable than others'. As the war in Iraq stretches towards its sixth year, we can no longer deny this fact. It might mean something that in this same class, the students believe that Barack Obama is half-Muslim.

Growing up, I loved those Chuck Norris films, too. We all did, and still do. But a complex alchemy happens when we watch those movies. When we cheer for Chuck Norris to kick the bad guy's ass, we become Chuck and the bad guy becomes America, or sometimes another ethnicity or group. The truth is that when the credits roll, no matter how we felt during the film, we are all left holding or dealing the cards of American foreign policy. We outsiders would like you to stop advertising your freedom to us and instead draft real and moral foreign policy. As I tell all my writing students: show, don't tell.

Part of the problem is that the excess of American culture makes it possible to erase in a relatively short period the memory of such things as the Great Depression. Americans have forgotten what it means to live with war, with occupation. Even 9/11 doesn't apply. I am not belittling the event at all by saying that most Americans (New Yorkers aside) experienced that trauma from a distance. It is not the same as a generation of Bosnians who remember snipers taking out their friends and siblings as they walked to school. Perhaps if the war came to American homes and streets, you would have been less cavalier about not impeaching a man whose decisions have produced the deaths of hundreds of thousands of people and cost his own country immeasurably, and yet rush to impeach a man for a sexual misdemeanor. Priorities.

7.

While attending the world economic forum in Davos earlier this year, I was amazed at how many Americans expressed concern over China's involvement in Africa and were scandalized by their possible abuse of the continent and its people. This despite the fact that the CIA has been behind every coup and countercoup in the continent's history; that the same CIA taught my country's torturers. This despite the fact that Americans watched Biafrans starve to death because, according to Lyndon B. Johnson, America couldn't afford the expense of saving Africa, as it did Japan and Europe after World War II. Americans watched while Rwandans were murdered and stood by and watched the Sudanese genocide. American oil companies continue to pillage the continent, creating dependent economies, and have done everything in their power to stall the formation of the African Union. Yet Americans are worried about China's involvement in Africa. For me, China's interest in Africa, clearly built on a model of mutual exploitation, has shaken America awake. As a result, the last American president toured the continent promising a pittance toward the AIDS epidemic while trying to strong-arm countries to allow American military bases. Will it ultimately lead to a more collaborative America and a less dictatorial one? This can bode well only for the smaller nations.

8.

If America truly wants to change its image, then it needs to confront and excise the specter of racism and sexism (even Pakistan has twice had a female prime minister). It needs to write and implement foreign policy driven by ethics, not expediency. America has to accept the humanity of the rest of the world.

Flagging Multiculturalism: How American Insularity Morally Justifies Itself

Uzma Aslam Khan

In the fall of 2005, waiting in the main hall of Grand Central Station in New York City, I glanced up at the ceiling dotted with stars. An enormous American flag dangled from the artificial sky, veiling the constellations. It seemed an apt finale to my two-month visit to the region: in Connecticut almost every yard had a flag, and it was not uncommon to see three or more. Public spaces had also been bombarded with the image. Whether I walked to the market or rode the bus to the library, the way was plastered with flags. Now here I was, gazing up at a model of our shared universe, but all I could see was the Star-Spangled Banner. I said as much to my American friend waiting with me for the train. She appeared not to see the flag (nor the smaller ones all around) and replied indignantly, "I believe in live and let live."

By then, over two years into the invasion of Iraq, the United States had dropped tens of thousands of cluster bombs on the country, containing millions of submunitions. Human Rights Watch had consistently warned that ground-launched cluster munitions were being used in areas heavily populated by civilians. The Iraqi death toll was estimated at more than five hundred thousand; up to two million Iraqis were believed homeless. For an American to refuse to see why a non-American considers the flag a symbol of "live and let die" is more than an oversight. It is a rejection of any parallels between us and them. It is a denial of a shared universe.

During that summer, my conversations about the richest country in the world bombing the poorest, Afghanistan; or bombing one of the most secular countries in the Islamic world, Iraq; or funneling nearly two billion dollars annually to Pakistan's military regime to fight the "war on terror" all ended with similar pat dismissals, like brushing away a pesky mosquito. Apart from being called "so self-righteous," and being told "live and let live" or "thanks for the insight," I encountered another way of swatting the bug of "insight" further out of earshot: my companions would first condemn the Bush administration (easily done). They would then follow this with a comment that increasingly sounds to me like an American national anthem: "Well, we're *all* victims."

This is what I was really being told by men and women, heterosexuals and homosexuals, blacks and whites, old and young, Christians and Jews, all educated professionals with an annual income roughly forty times that of the nonindustrialized world that lives in terror of being targeted by U.S. wrath: *I've been there.*

This flag is a great conversation stopper. It is the flag to end all flags.

It means *I* am exceptional because *I* suffered and *I* survived. But when every American subscribes to what can only be called a cult of victimhood, where is exception? Where is diversity?

To my mind, U.S. foreign policy aside, it is this that most alienates non-Americans from Americans: no matter how wealthy, steadily employed, ensconced in comfortable neighborhoods, well fed, healthy, and well educated they are; no matter how lavish their lifestyle—coolly consuming far more than their share of the world's natural resources with complete impunity; no matter how much they have, most Americans think of themselves as deprived. The reason is always "history," but the relationship with history is rarely a correspondence with something beyond oneself. It is rarely one of connectedness: few of the Irish-Americans who complain of "No Irish Need Apply" signs have been turned away from jobs themselves; few living Greek Americans had to flee the Turks; even fewer Catholic Americans have suffered Protestant persecution; Polish Americans have long since bid adieu to Stalin. These communities don't provide the only examples: there are countless others.

This is not to say that in America the playing field is level. Far from it. Nor is it to disparage historical traumas. It is to point out that many of the people who most vociferously recall these and other historical wrongs have never lived through them, and in fact enjoy, by global standards, extremely affluent and coddled lives. Past injustice is often cited by this vast American socioeconomic bracket as a justification for blamelessness in the present. Inevitably, citations are spun using pop-psychological terms such as *persecution*, *addiction*, *recovery*, and *redemption*. Instead of connectedness and debate, the relationship with history is more often one of isolation and entitlement. Entitlement to more affluence, more therapy, more drugs, more addictions, more redemption, more isolation—and more entitlement.

In times of war and international censure, victimhood is America's immunity from blame. It is a moral missile-defense shield.

Art, like history, is a commitment to something beyond oneself. It allows us to be, in John Berger's words, "more deeply inserted into existence than the course of a single life would have us believe." Surely, to be more deeply inserted into existence, our defenses must be shed.

Since the 2003 Iraq War, with the growing international furor against the illegal detention and torture of prisoners in Iraq, Afghanistan, Pakistan, and Guantánamo Bay, and with the unpopularity of threats to attack Iran and even Pakistan (America's ally for all sixty years of its life), the American empire's moral missile-defense shield has been chipped. You would think that art would aid in this process. You would think that the kinds of factual and fictional stories coming from the part of the world being "bombed to the middle ages," or close to it, would, through dignity and insight, inventiveness and an ability to evoke wonder, chip harder at the shell. This is not happening.

In fact, the stories from predominantly Islamic countries that prove most popular with Westerners are designed to make the defense shield even more impenetrable. Take, for instance, the hysteria with which "life narratives" by "Muslim women" are being consumed. The titles are mouthwatering: *My Forbidden Face* by Latifa (Afghan woman's "true story"); *Choke on Your Lies* by Inci Y. (Turkish-German woman is forced to marry a man in Turkey); *Married by Force* by Leila (Moroccan-French girl is, who knew, married by force); *Princess* by Jean Sasson (unnamable Saudi princess reveals herself). These "authentic" memoirs all come packaged in the same cover: a woman gazing out in terror from behind a burqa of soft lilac or pure black. This is the most eagerly consumed image of the Islamic world, more popular even than the image of the bearded terrorist. For the image of woman-in-burqa signifies both: the terrorist and the victim. It reinforces fear of *them* and redeems trust in *us*. It gives war a moral justification: the emancipation of the Muslim woman. After all, when bombs fall on veiled women, the veils fall off.

Never mind that there are more than five hundred million Muslim women in the world today (almost twice the number of Americans), from cultures as diverse as the Ivory Coast and Indonesia, speaking thousands of different languages, dressed in everything from skirts to saris to sarongs, in colors more vibrant than a coral reef, and with histories just as multicultural as the kaleidoscope Americans claim only for themselves. Such a woman may not even group herself along any racial, religious, or gender lines, preferring a more secular, universal identity (for instance, human). In arrogant disregard of the complex layers of her identity, she is only ever depicted as the veiled icon from Saudi Arabia or Afghanistan.

The icon does not reflect her. It predicts her. It tags her, turns her into a known product. There is a warning on her label: nothing new inside. And there is a promise: peek behind the burqa and find deliciously sordid details of abuse and rape, all "real."

Needless to say, these books are not read for artistic technique. In fact, it has been suggested to me on numerous occasions in numerous countries (from the United States to Portugal to, sadly, my own, Pakistan) that *real* women writers from my part of the world (read: Muslim) cannot afford to work on style. The *real* ones are so preoccupied with escaping the drudgery of their lives that they can barely get a few words down, let alone concern themselves with how they are written. I beg to differ: a writer's lifework is developing and staying true to her aesthetic, period. If she has to fight to do it—and in Pakistan, she will have to fight: to study; to speak; to have privacy; to afford privacy; to put her work first, even over her family; to see into doors that are closed to her for political, social, economic, and make-believe religious reasons; the list goes on—then she has to fight to do it.

But *Princess* and *My Forbidden Face* are read with as much fervor in the East as in the West. They just as frequently deck the bookshops of Lahore and Dubai as Antwerp and Tucson. So here's the additional rub: having reduced all Muslim women to the one dimension of the veiled icon, the western mind assumes the authority to speak for them as a group and know what they want (*our* freedom), while the eastern imagination also buys it! Western-dominated images of the East are increasingly absorbed by the eastern imagination, which feeds them back to the West.

Thus the global reader is also promised—along with the thrill of slumming—an opportunity to participate in the hackneyed portrayal, believing (and I have actually heard this said) that with each book sale, the Muslim woman comes closer to emancipation and, that ultimate promise, *recovery.* Life narratives about Muslim women provide an even better way of shrugging off the shamefulness of war: in addition to having his or her position of advantage affirmed, the consumer gets to play the savior and thus feels vindicated.

A particularly ghoulish example of this form of group emancipation therapy occurred a few months before 9/11, when Eve Ensler invited Zoya, a representative of the Revolutionary Association of the Women of Afghanistan (RAWA), to Madison Square Garden in New York. The event was Ensler's performance of her play *The Vagina Monologues.* Tickets were $1,000 per head. After the play, Oprah Winfrey read Ensler's poem, "Under the Burqa." For dramatic effect, Zoya was made to appear under a shuttlecock burqa. Oprah recited: "Imagine a huge dark piece of cloth / hung over your entire body / like you were a shameful statue. . . . " All the lights were switched off but for one. This fell on Zoya, who, per her orders, walked slowly up the stage. Then, at last, Oprah *lifted the burqa off.* The crowd leaped to their feet, applauding merrily. Eighteen thousand wealthy Americans (including those of eastern descent) got to fantasize about being "persecuted." They got to play the liberator. We're all victims and survivors, right? And as reward, Zoya got to speak about the brutality of life under the Taliban—for a full two minutes. (For details of Zoya's spectacular ascent from hell to heaven, see the *Nation*, March 5, 2001.)

RAWA is a well-known and well-respected organization all over the world. Genuine respect for the courage with which all Afghan women daily battle the gruesome reality of living under the Taliban would have involved Zoya's addressing the crowd without having to make a spectacle of herself. No one would have presumed to represent or liberate her.[1] I have to believe that this is what some men and women in the audience (an audience that was predominantly female) would have wanted. They did not ask for the spectacle. They were there that day for Ensler's play; Zoya was a sideshow. If her American hosts wanted to take an honest part in her story, and if they wanted the audience to do the same, then they would have lowered their defenses by speaking of America's role in creating the Taliban.

Even today, few Americans are willing to acknowledge that the Taliban as born in the vacuum that was left after

---

1. In Gillian Whitlock's book *Soft Weapons: Autobiography in Transit* (Chicago: The University of Chicago Press, 2007), Zoya is quoted as describing the event thus: "I had been asked to wear my burqa, and the light streamed through the mesh in front of my face and brought tears to my eyes....I had to climb some steps, but because of the burqa and the tears in my eyes, I had to be helped up the stairs. Slowly, very slowly Oprah lifted the burqa off me and let it fall to the stage." While some may argue that Zoya does not make explicit that she felt humiliated, it is clear that she was told to wear the burqa for the purpose of being liberated by a Western woman.

the Islamic Jihad, funded by the United States, fought the Soviet Union with western arms from 1979 until 1989. During this period, "Islamists" were the good guys: Ronald Reagan compared them to America's founding fathers. They won praise from the U.S. media, academics, and ordinary Americans, or at least from those who had heard of Afghanistan or Islam at all. Instead of making Zoya parade in a burqa, her hosts could have expressed sorrow that she and other Afghans would not have had to live under the Taliban (and continue to live under them) had the United States not abandoned Afghanistan after it helped "win" the Cold War. This would have been *shared experience*. This would have been closer to poetry. Instead, Ensler, who is Jewish, and Winfrey, who is black, being minority women themselves, felt entitled to co-opt Zoya's struggle, humiliating her in the bargain. To my mind, they came closer to enacting the Taliban than enacting fantasies of pain and rescue.

Step into the past for a moment and imagine the reverse, for I know of no better way to communicate the offense: Can anyone picture Ensler or Winfrey arriving in Afghanistan decked in Auschwitz uniforms or slave shackles, for Afghan women to "visualize" their pain and express sympathy by pulling off the clothes or releasing the chains? The very image is repugnant. Then why is the image of an Afghan woman being made to parade in *her* chains not equally disgraceful? Why not accept that people everywhere have equal dignity? "Live and let live" is indeed a fine philosophy—but it does not mean much if you compel someone to eat from your hand.

One wonders what's next. Will an Abu Ghraib prisoner be led into a New York arena with weights dangling from his testicles so Americans can see what it's like before Jay Leno unsaddles him?

Zoya's unveiling in New York came in the wake of her autobiography, *Zoya's Story.* Since 9/11, her book, like so many other "true stories" from the Islamic world, has flown off the shelves. Though her story is vital, it has been turned into propaganda. Apart from justifying the ongoing wars, it helps the West forget its long and often ugly presence in the region.

Works of fiction are fulfilling a similar purpose. Take, for instance, Khaled Hosseini's hugely successful *The Kite Runner.* Here the West is shown liberating the East when an Afghan American returns to Afghanistan to save the son of his childhood servant. Given the decades of war that Afghans have endured, often while the world looked away, it is a shame that Hosseini's liberator did not come from within. Instead, the liberator is an American minority, affirming America's multicultural self-image. The book makes no mention of the U.S. role in creating the Taliban or reinforcing its cause in the post–9/11 world of the story's beginning and end. In Hosseini's second novel, *A Thousand Splendid Suns,* a violent man marries and abuses first one young girl, then another. It, too, is set during the Soviet occupation of Afghanistan and the country's subsequent Talibanization. Once again it skirts the U.S. occupation. Once again the women inspire pity and horror rather than empathy and remorse. They serve to reinforce America's moral missile-defense shield.

Whether in autobiography or in fiction, the image of the passive Muslim woman nicely bridges the twin impressions that America has of the world that lies somewhere out there, somewhere east and south of Greece. Seen through one lens, Muslims are dangerous and must be ruled. Through the other, they are pitiful and must be saved. The image of the passive Muslim woman also feeds into the twin impressions that America has of itself: We are victims; we are self-liberated. It is in this image that both worldviews are affirmed and united.

Writers and artists from the Islamic world and the Third World that present different worldviews—ones in which women and men are not easily defined; ones in which no race, religion, or nation is portrayed as more on the side of freedom than any other—are seldom read or heard.

For dissent to be heard, it must come from within the United States, or at least from within North America or Europe. Would, say, Noam Chomsky or George Monbiot enjoy the same worldwide readership if he were from Afghanistan, Iraq, or Iran? There's no doubt that we sorely need the Chomskys and Monbiots of the West, but the fact remains that they are read far more than anti-imperialist voices from the East, who are either ignored or dismissed as reactionaries—even by their own countries—unless they immigrate to the West, thus affirming western multiculturalism and tolerance. I would argue that this is especially true for women.

Unless she goes Zoya's way and lets herself be "saved," a woman from the East who lives in the East is unlikely to be heard over the multicultural trumpeting of the West, particularly if she is Muslim. Nor is she likely to be heard at home, over the political and social turmoil around her, particularly if she is unreal enough to value style as much as content.

Which raises a final point. A writer's impulse is that of a child: to explore the world, to move beyond doors that are closed, regardless of who closes them. Will there come a time when writers from the East are read not to see "how they see us, in the West" but "how they see *beyond* us"? A free East will be possible only when the Eastern imagination stops relying on Western-dominated global literary trends and starts to feed itself.

Now for a thoroughly enjoyable example of dissent from within the United States (never mind, for a moment, that we might not have heard about it if had come from where I live):

In the Letters section of the September 2002 issue of *Harper's Magazine*, in response to an article by the late Palestinian-American writer Edward Said, a reader bemoaned the "cultural stagnation of the Arab world." As proof, he cited the following from a United Nations Development Program report: "The entire Arab world, with a population of 280 million, translates only about 330 books per year." Two months later, a witty letter counterargued that, since the number of translations was being hailed as the indicator of a culture's dynamism, the following statistic is also noteworthy: "Here in the United States, at the cosmopolitan heart of the universe, with a population of 285 million and a publishing industry that churns out well over 100,000 books per year, we publish—well, what do you know—about 330 books in translation per year."

The statistic begs the question: Does the United States disparage non-Western cultures because it fears confronting a frighteningly authentic equality? Is xenophobia in fact not a fear of differences but of similarities? To step outside the moral missile-defense shield is to see oneself as, after all, not much freer, safer, more tolerant, or more multicultural than *them*.

In November 2007, the *Guardian* reported that the Arab world was finally paying attention to its shoddy translation record by initiating Kalima, an Abu Dhabi–based translation project. Among the "great works of world literature" on its list was *The Kite Runner*.

The article mentioned a British author acknowledging the influence of the Arab civilization on the subsequent European Renaissance, but no one mentioned the cost to education and culture brought about by the British and American invasion of Iraq, such as the gutting of Baghdad's libraries. Close to a million publications in Arabic, Farsi, Turkish, and Kurdish, as well as in English, French, Spanish, Italian, and German, including rare manuscripts and ancient texts, have been lost. The Central Library of Baghdad University is still in ashes. Offers to help rebuild it have not come from the UK or USA but from Japan. Kalima's plan to translate five hundred titles a year into Arabic by 2010 was called "a cause for great celebration," but no one mentioned how many great works of world literature the United States plans on translating into English and publishing by 2010.

Any guesses?

Giving the Harness Bells a Shake

Mourid Barghouti

In one of his early articles, the distinguished American poet W. S. Merwin writes: "Where injustice prevails (and where does it not?) a poet . . . has no choice but to name the wrong as truthfully as he can, and to try to indicate the claims of justice in terms of the victims he lives among."

I agree and would add that American intellectuals, writers, and journalists who try to "name the wrong as truthfully as they can" are part of humanity's thirst for justice and independent thinking. American forms of popular protest and the vibrant discussions within American society assert the fact that the concept of *us*, exactly as the concept of *them*, has never been and will never be an inert lifeless block. An overly simple consensus on the meaning of the two pronouns *we* and *they* must not be allowed. They should not be used as labels for sweeping generalizations. On our small planet, no race, no culture, no ethnicity or religion is a guest. The present civilization, the outcome of the contributions of all cultures, is the shared property of all mankind.

I witnessed the fall of the Berlin Wall and the end of the Soviet Empire. I lived in Budapest and saw the elation of millions and their great expectations for a happier future. The United States of America became the single superpower on earth and was left to lead the world community without any rival. It did it very badly, persisting in its aggressive, interventionist policies as the long-armed world policeman in Asia, Africa, Latin America, and the Middle East, expanded its military bases throughout the world and lightly sent young men and women to war. The "War on Terror" has become a tool to end opposition to local dictators and to demonize legitimate resistance movements. The United States has resorted to the self-deceptive trick of being reactive; its leaders refuse to investigate the causes of those resistance movements—that is, the military occupation in Palestine, Iraq, and Afghanistan. The White House has devoted itself to stifling any voice calling for an international conference to discuss a globally agreed-upon definition of *terrorism*. Its unilateralism has almost destroyed the fabric of the United Nations, which is supposed to be the world's arbitrator. America has become the judge, jury, and executioner. And now millions have taken to the streets around the world, protesting American policies and wars. These huge antiwar demonstrations should have startled many in the United States because they came less than two years after the near-universal outpouring of support and sympathy for the American people in the aftermath of the crime of September 11, 2001.

Americans' present preoccupation with the question "how do they see us?" is perfectly justified. And from my part of the world, the answer would be: "Very well."

We see you very well, from *Friends* to F-16s, from rock 'n' roll to "Shock and Awe," from Walt Whitman to white phosphorus, from the Museum of Modern Art to Guantánamo, from Michael Moore to Fox News, from John Kennedy to George W. Bush, and from Donald Duck to Donald Rumsfeld, whose groundbreakingly original vanguard poetry many can recite by heart:

> As we know, there are known knowns. There are things we know we know. We also know there are known unknowns. That is to say we know there are some things we do not know. But there are also unknown unknowns, the ones we don't know we don't know.

We live in the American Age. An American tourist or resident in Arab countries need not abandon any facet of his or her lifestyle: he or she would fly *American Airlines* in a *Boeing*, go to *Avis* rent-a-car and take a *Ford* or *Chevrolet* to a *Hilton* or *Sheraton* where his room's minibar would be stuffed with *Coca-Cola*, *Pepsi Cola*, *Bounty*, and *Mars*, stopping by a *McDonald's* restaurant, paying it all with a *Visa* credit card or *American Express* traveler checks or cash withdrawal from any *Citibank* branch. America travels with Americans and returns with them on the same flight. America is everywhere.

In my part of the world, however, the question might be of a different nature: "Do they see us?" Or, "Does America see us at all?" Do you hear our voice? As a matter of fact, despite having the best intelligence agencies, news agencies and correspondents, academic think tanks and research centers, Ivy League universities and 154,000 troops in our midst, you do not see us. It seems to me that America wants to see and hear America, and thinks that this is sufficient. One of my poetry collections has the title *The Logic of All Beings*. This book is composed of epigrams in which people, plants, animals, and things speak:

The mirror said:
How miserable I am,
No one of those looking at me
Wants to see "me"

A common nightmare is one in which the dreamer seems to want to say something, to scream, to explain, but the voice is stifled, lost. I think there are whole groups, communities, peoples, races, and languages that face that traumatic experience of the blocked scream, their voices strangled either by local tyrannies or by being ignored by the outside world. Ninety percent of world languages are absent from the Internet. Arabic literature both classical and modern, though with an unbroken continuity for fifteen hundred years, is almost absent from the world stage, especially in the United States, where readers think that we have no literature except for Kahlil Gibran and the *Arabian Nights*. The dominant culture of our present times, which has been able to discover, observe, and understand the secrets of the body as well as the secrets of the universe, is also the culture that is oblivious to other languages, discourses, and civilizations. The rulers of the single unrivaled superpower seem to be afraid and suspicious of the rest of the world, and the rest of the world is afraid and suspicious of the Pentagon's future wars. If the USA insists on being the single legislator of right and wrong, good and evil, if it insists on the us-vs.-them division of humanity, then our world will grow more dangerous.

Does America hold a mirror to see others? Does she think of what she sees, or does she always see what she thinks? When you are the single superpower on this planet, you are easily tempted to define others, to label them, and to think of them as one unit. We do see the diversity of the American people: we see their achievements, talents, inventions, movies, novels, shows, songs, dances, and love stories as well as the abuses of soldiers in the corridors of Abu Ghraib and the aggressive policies and machinations of their successive administrations, Republican or Democrat. Whenever our fanatics and fundamentalists label America "evil," they are faced down by those who remind them of the "other" America, the beautiful America. That is not because we are wiser or more objective, but because your two sides are completely visible to us and widely reported, discussed, and professionally studied. On the other hand, we are victims of systematic, incessant disinformation and misinformation that aim to highlight our mistakes (and we have a lot of them, just as you do). A Palestinian, an Arab, or a Moslem is never depicted as a human being, a lover, painter, engineer, neighbor, uncle, a man, or a woman with a sense of humor, who would sometimes tell a small lie or cheat on a school exam or even cheat on a spouse— that is, a normal creature just like all others.

Is it colonial blindness that guides White House policy toward our region? Or is it a desire to resort to military might and the power of the media to impose the American will everywhere? Yes, the media can be a training camp for injustice and a tool in global domination. The Pentagon needs Fox News and other powerful cultural figures, and they complement one another. The empire needs its docile talking heads.

Our problem is that the single greatest power in the world and Europe are blindly supporting Israel and are totally biased in their attitude toward the Middle East. The American elite automatically adopt the Israeli narrative and refuse to acknowledge our rights or suffering. The USA (and Europe) seem to think that anything done or decided by Israel is good, legal, and legitimate: the collective punishment, the settlement-building, the apartheid wall, the targeted killings, the denial of the Right to Return of the Palestinian refugees, the re-re-reoccupation of our towns and villages, and the military checkpoints and incarceration of more than eleven thousand Palestinians in Israeli detention centers and jails . . . the list goes on. With such a bias you can never reach a just solution, and it is this bias that is the real obstacle to successful negotiations or a lasting peace in the region.

I do wish that some American columnists, TV commentators, editors, and filmmakers were similar to some of their Israeli colleagues. Yes, even the Israeli press is far better. We are being systematically demonized by both sides, but pro-Israeli American Media is more fanatically pro-Israeli than the Israelis themselves.

Is this caused by historic misunderstanding? This question is serious indeed because it stands as a euphemism for biased policies. I was once asked in an interview about the misunderstanding of Islam in the United States and in the West in general. This was my answer:

> If "misunderstanding" serves some people's interests and helps in the achievement of their objectives they will *decide to misunderstand*. Misunderstanding, here, is not an incident of bad luck or the lack of information and data; it is an *intentional choice*.

Political leaders and biased mass media are skilled at elevating certain values and concepts or degrading them to the lowest abyss, according to their agenda. The whole thing is not about disputed theological or cultural differences or philosophical issues. One has to look for political economy to understand the attempts of the decision makers in the USA to impose uniform global values on all nations and all cultures. The neoconservatives' language of *us* vs. *them* can lead to endless wars and send humans to the killing fields. Scandalous paradoxes and aggressive, deceptive propaganda subject our world to the terrorism the rest of the world claims to fight.

Democracy is accepted or rejected according to Washington's interests; dictatorships are created, armed, financed, and protected by Washington in one region and bombarded with smart bombs in another. Unfortunately,

America was and is the main friend, protector, and supporter of any dictator in the world serving its interests, from the royal family in Saudi Arabia to General Pinochet in Chile to Musharraf in Pakistan. You cannot ally with such dictators and then invade other countries to teach democracy.

Will such policies continue? Almost all Arab countries are now ruled by dictatorships and corrupt governments. Millions of Arabs are economic emigrants outside their countries. Millions more are in voluntary exile. The life of those who stay in their countries is not easier. Political prisoners in Arab jails number in the thousands, and the United States is allied with their oppressors. American alliances in this part of the world protract our suffering.

The Israeli military occupation has been turning Palestinian life into a real hell, and it will continue to do so because of the small thinking of the Israeli government and its biggest friend, the USA. In fact, all destructive theories such as fascism, racism, apartheid, colonialism, terrorism, despotism are the result of small thinking and oversimplification of complex issues. Israel and the USA refuse to see the humanity of their victims, and until this attitude changes, the so-called "peace process" and all attempts to solve the problem will end in failure. The Palestinians have been negotiating with Israel for fifteen years now in the framework of the "peace process" without achieving anything, and that is partly because of the unconditional American support of Israel's intransigence and its contempt for international law. By putting pressure on the weak side in the conflict, the USA can achieve some accord and celebrate success, but this will

not last. It might postpone tensions or delay confronta-
tions, but without justice, no agreement or accord can
survive and no crisis can be solved.

I am not a politician and it is too late for me to become
one. I have never joined any political party and I will
not do so now, but it is my duty to name the wrong as
truthfully as I can and to point out injustices perpetrated
by any side. It is my duty to put the two pronouns *us*
and *them* under scrutiny and to be critical of "our" own
actions and reactions as Arabs and Moslems.

Hysterical calls to condemn anything American are
the product of second-rate analysis and miserable oversimplification. Such calls are part of the problem and not
part of the solution. Fortunately, this is not the dominant
trend. Our students do their best to join American universities, and we enjoy the fruits of American creativity
and explorations in arts, sciences, social studies, and technology. But U.S. military boots on our soil are strongly
opposed, and our independence will not be broken to
please American corporations. George W. Bush's feeble
attempt to understand anti-American sentiment led him
to announce that *they envy us.* This pseudoanalysis of
international conflicts is dim-witted complacency that
explains nothing. What should be said to the American
people is that we do not envy you for your way of life,
but we reject taking other peoples' lives to keep your way
of life. Any terrorist answer to conflicts is equally rejected.
On September 11, 2001, the whole world was united in
genuine sympathy and solidarity with the USA. There
was no reason for the Bush administration to fabricate

lies and concoct false evidence about "weapons of mass destruction" and plunge into a devastating war.

Aware of its bad image in the Middle East, where anti-American sentiments run high, the Bush administration has set up the Arabic-language satellite network Al-Hurra, Radio Sawa, and strengthened ties with many local journalists, newspapers, and magazines to win the hearts and minds of the people, but none of these efforts appear to have achieved substantial results. The mission to promote American policies would be easier if these policies were subjected to serious reassessment. You cannot maintain such aggressive and biased policies and expect to improve the way you are seen in the region. The faith in military power has plagued the foreign policy of the United States. But a military solution to all conflicts and differences is not only dangerous and costly; it is futile and more than that, inevitably leads to new conflicts. History tells us that neither the powerful remain powerful forever, nor do the weak remain weak forever.

Has the time of serious reassessment come with Obama? Does he really mean change when he says change? Of course this remains to be seen, but as there are limits to power there are also limits for change in the United States of America. Unlike many U.S. presidents, Obama has come to the White House from the sphere of intellect, reading, writing, knowing his people and the world (he is not the military Eisenhower, the peanut fields Carter, the oil industry Bush to name just three), but he also has come from the culture of the Civil Rights movement and his promise is so great that the whole world gave a sigh of relief and received him with hope, admiration and wide expectations. His first remarks and political moves towards the Middle East showed maximum caution and a studied ambiguity, which could be seen here as a graceful withdrawal from his promises of change. What we see is not a new course but an attempt to improve an existing one. This is not enough.

A full withdrawal from Iraq is a great step forward, yet a surge in troops in Afghanistan should not be seen as a necessary price. Sending more troops to Afghanistan will endanger more lives, American and Afghani alike, and is not likely to bear any more political fruits than foreign military occupations elsewhere in the region. With regard to the Arab-Israeli conflict, President Obama will do well to keep in mind this basic fact: the core of that conflict is Occupation. Israeli occupation of the Palestinian land must end. The obscene peace process has been used for nineteen years, ever since Madrid Conference, as a tool to facilitate Israeli settlement building, confiscation of territory, and constructing the apartheid separation which resulted in a full fledged apartheid regime forced on the Palestinian people. Palestinians in the occupied territories have been denied their civil and political rights for more than forty years. They are being ruled by laws they never got the chance to vote for or against. Arab citizens of Israel have at least one right less than Jewish citizens; the right of return. If the four million Palestinian refugees were to turn Jewish tomorrow, they would be given that right. Promoting liberal ideas of secularism and human equality is unlikely to flourish if millions of people are under the impression that they have been kept in tents for sixty years only because they have the wrong religion.

In one of his pre-election rallies Obama emphasized that there were no blue or red states in America. The United States of Martin Luther King, however, is different from the United States of George W. Bush, and Obama still has a lot of work to do if he wants to change the world. A compromised equality is no equality at all.

Wild-Blooded Envoys of the Future

Victor Erofeyev

A Visit to a Museum

The small pregnant woman, who somehow reminded me of Andrei Bolkonsky's wife—the one who died in childbirth in *War and Peace*—assembled the group of about a dozen Russians in front of a picture by Cezanne. The blonde American smiled at us with a well-studied, ingenuous smile that was intended to hold our interest at least until the end of the tour, introduced herself, and plunged into the dark waters of the unknown. The one thing she did know about this group was that she was facing high-priority VIPs who had come to the Museum of Modern Art by special arrangement with the management, outside normal hours, before the museum was officially open. Which meant that the interaction between people and pictures would be exclusively intimate and intense, a genuine New York gala performance. Apart from the security men there was no one else in the exhibition halls. But what were these people standing in front of her like, how badly did they want to experience this close interaction with Cezanne's clearly inedible apples? The most definite thing one could say about the members of this cultural incursion was that they were not hungry. Before coming to the museum, they had eaten a solid breakfast in their expensive hotel, consuming huge, bright-colored omelettes with tomatoes, mushrooms, and ham, and they were in a genial mood. The small pregnant woman tried to get a feel for their level. She explained that Paul Cezanne was a French artist of the late nineteenth century. This information was received with due appreciation and that seemed to encourage her somewhat. These people standing in front of her were well groomed, on the young side, and had a general air, if not of affluence, then at least of calm self-confidence, a certain aroma that united them all. Actually, they were united by certain other aromas as well. There was a sense in which they were collectors of aromas—the odors of delicious food, the latest perfumes and lotions, horses, stylish automobiles, a multitude of drinks. In fact, it was the aroma and taste of a drink that had brought them here to New York, for the world premiere of a twenty-year-old whisky—the launch of an expensive product that was set to conquer the world. The gastronomic connection between Cezanne's apples and this still-unfamiliar but archetypically superb whisky was glimmering elusively in the mist.

The small pregnant woman gradually grew bolder. She began to believe in the Russian group and cast aside the cultural crutches required for Texas billionaires, confidently piling on the special terms. The group surged onward to storm the bastions of cubism and abstract art. On the way to victory, however, the group began to fragment. Claude Monet's meters-wide canvases of waterlilies, which are usually impossible to see properly because of crowds, met with approval, but Picasso's *Demoiselles d'Avignon*, who turned out to be common Barcelona prostitutes, evoked conflicting responses. Salvador Dalí won the group over, but more with his reputation than his subjects. As far as the Russian brigade was concerned, the great battle between Picasso and Dalí was definitely not won by the pop-eyed innovator who joined the Communist Party, but by Lorca's treacherous executor, the man who sang a hymn of praise to prison as the great repository of freedom. These Spanish competitors were both devotees of the erotic. But Picasso's eroticism was the lust of a robustly healthy spirit, while Dalí's surrealist pictures were filled with a creeping perversion that evoked a sweet tremor of revulsion.

The small pregnant woman concluded the tour on a patriotic note—in the American hall. But when it came to American abstract artists like Jackson Pollock, several women in the Russian group said something for which Khruschev would have loved them: We could paint better than that. The small pregnant woman didn't argue, she didn't even purse her lips in an expression of scorn: she was used to everything. The visit to the museum had taken place. The group hurried off to lunch in a swanky restaurant.

A Beautiful Woman

On the way to the restaurant I phoned Anka. A mechanical American woman informed me that her number had changed and dictated a new series of digits. When

Anka, a beautiful forty-seven-year-old ex-Muscovite, first received her American passport, she couldn't believe her eyes: the American authorities had confused a seven with a one and made her six years younger. She jumped for joy. But this time when I flew to New York, she couldn't be bothered to meet up with me, claiming that she was feeling depressed and unwell.

"Living in America is the ultimate punishment for me," Anka said on the phone.

She had begun her life in New York by moving into a fashionable building on Broadway, where she and her husband had two apartments knocked into one. He was a classical pianist and she flew around the world with him, first class all the way. They mingled with the upper crust of society. Her wardrobes were bursting with fur coats, and she never wore the same pair of shoes twice. And then they got divorced and she moved to a rather less chic apartment close to Central Park. Following unsuccessful financial ventures and a robbery, she was left with no means of support. She dreamed of getting married, but it didn't work out. Rich old men, brilliant tenors, and Washington politicians came flocking to her beauty like a flight of carrion crows, pecking and clawing at it before darting away again. Despite her society connections, she either couldn't find a job or didn't want to. And now she had moved again, closer to Harlem. This was where the idea of the ultimate punishment had been born.

"Find me a fiancé in Moscow," she said and hung up.

The Agent

In 1988, when I came to New York for the first time from Vermont, where I was lecturing on Russian literature, I started getting such terrible dizzy spells that it was a real effort for me to walk along the streets of Manhattan. I felt as if people here didn't walk; they whizzed along on roller skates with their ties fluttering in the breeze. I felt as if this was the only place where there was anything real going on, the place where a new breed of people was being born. My novel *Russian Beauty* had not yet made me famous, but already people were inviting me everywhere, asking me to write for *Vogue* and the *New Yorker*, taking me out to dinner with the legendary owner of these magazines and many others, introducing me to celebrities—Arthur Miller, Philip Roth—and all the while listening to my stories of the Soviet Union during the time of perestroika with genuine American enthusiasm. I couldn't understand what was happening, why New York had taken me to its heart in this way. I was taken to the Twin Towers to admire the view from the high-level bar. On the way back to my hotel I always felt like the impostor Khlestakov from Gogol's *Dead Souls*.

I started traveling to New York more and more often on assignments for various non-Russian magazines. I wrote about Harlem and nightclubs, drug addicts and policemen, schools and prisons, sadists and university professors, transvestites and feminists. New York was transformed into a fuzzy cloud of pink candyfloss on a stick. I kept eating it and I just couldn't get enough. Eventually I acquired a literary agent, one of the finest in New York, who sold his authors for megabucks and was a Hollywood insider. To me, he seemed like the very incarnation of fame and success, a wizard, a conjuror, an American shaman. He launched me into orbit.

New York ended the day that those crazy Arabs ploughed their planes into the Twin Towers. I arrived in October, six weeks after the terrorist attack. The city that usually smells of hot dogs still had a powerful odor of roasted human flesh. Everyone was wearing patriotic badges with the American flag, but the badges didn't help. Americans are not good at enduring calamity, although they know how to distract themselves from it. But in a country where the only possible answer to the question "How are things?" is "Fine!" it's impossible to find any answer to global catastrophe.

New York is the city of yellow taxis. Everyone knows that, if only from the movies. Before the catastrophe, the New York taxi drivers liked to talk about why they came to America from their own countries—Russia, Brazil, Afghanistan, Bangladesh. These immigrants were nimble, quick on their feet, in a hurry to make money. But now it was if they'd put on weight and the effort of making money was a real strain. Against the background of changes that had taken place the day the Twins were killed, our Russian team that had come here to drink whisky looked so elegant and optimistic that the Americans might have specially arranged our presence to remind themselves of forgotten national values. The austerity that originally derived from puritanism led to New York's becoming an immense working city. When the Russian group hired a yacht to view New York from the water, what it saw was not a dream-city, but a gigantic snail that had withdrawn into itself. But there was still a special occasion waiting for us out on the waterway: the Statue of Liberty remained imperturbable. Perhaps it will be the cure that will allow the American nation to carry on. When they saw it, the Russian brigade raised their glasses. After we took a few swallows, the statue livened up a bit. We all clearly saw it dancing a jig.

When evening came the Russian group set off for another astounding restaurant and I was able to invite my agent along. He brought the writer Robert Greene, famous for the books in which he has rewritten world history in the American style, identifying only one motivation in life from ancient Egypt to modern Japan: the road to success. The writer's fiancée came, too. They got there before us and were sitting over their aperitifs.

And then for the first time I actually saw the striking difference between successful Americans and successful Russians. The setting for this comparison was a fashionable restaurant that every snob in New York would like to get into, but you have to book weeks in advance and it's excruciatingly expensive. The Russians arrived decked in their usual blaze of Italian splendor—which looks like a mockery of clothes or, perhaps, clothes designed to mock—and flopped onto their chairs as if they were sitting down in some simple sushi bar, without even realizing that they had invited three Americans. If they'd invited them, fine—no need to make a song and dance out of it. And in the Russians' company, the Americans, wearing their expensive jackets with silver buttons and respectable ties, looked like prim and proper English teachers at the annual office party. The Russians started downing mojitos with fresh mint leaves and complaining to each other that in New York they wouldn't sell one person more than five smartphones—it was just like the Soviet Union—so you couldn't make a gift of this crazy American technology to all your friends. My Americans hadn't even bought themselves one smartphone yet. But then, I still remember about those five smartphones per person, and I don't remember what I spoke about with the Americans. It must have been literature. Or democracy. And all the while the Russians grinned brightly and hedonistically, with captivatingly cultured smiles, although no one mentioned the visit to the museum even once, as if they had never even been there.

At the end of the evening, the Americans said that this had been a really special occasion for them. The Russians liked the restaurant, too, noting, "Even for Moscow, this place is high class." My agent asked me curiously, "Who are they?" And I said, "What do you mean? They're fine guys. Envoys of the future." I explained that in this Russian brigade I saw the core of the Russian world that was taking shape. Of course, some things would have to be sacrificed. You couldn't carry *Les Demoiselles d'Avignon* with you into this future. And we'd leave *The Brothers Karamazov* behind in the past, too. Culture simply has to become a garnish for life.

The Public Library

To surprise people, you have to shake their perceptions. Not so very long ago, Salman Rushdie arranged a party for writers from all around the world among the dinosaurs at the New York Natural History Museum. You might have got the idea that writers as a class had become dinosaurs, although in fact it was the dinosaurs who were roused by the din created by the fifteen-hundred-strong crowd.

The Scotch whisky command staff had decided to resurrect the past in their own way. They gave America something that had been taken away from it during the years of prohibition. They made the American elite a gift of a brand that was launched in 1909, during the great awakening of America. To discover your future, drink your glorious past! Envoys of national glamour were gathered from all round the world. The Japanese and Arabs and Chinese flew in, together with our own Russian assault battalion. It was a genuine birthday party, with a brass band, countless photographers, TV correspondents clutching microphones, and a guard of Scottish master bagpipers wearing kilts.

This was an object lesson in how to create a really special occasion. What are the essential elements for a global bash? The most important thing in a celebration like this is the ritualistic mystery of the event. It's a pyramid. There must be glimpses of superstars among the celebrities to get the whole hall excited, but the superstars themselves must be delighted by the appearance of the supreme echelon of society—blue-blooded members of the aristocracy. In this skirmish of the elite, the winner is not the democratically elected president, but the scion of the most ancient line. Then there is the gastronomic effect. The food must be recognizable and comprehensible to everyone but served like a culinary curve ball—off-the wall combinations like North-Sea crab and tropical papaya. The wines must be of impeccable listing, without any upstart pretensions, recognizable but not selected for whimsy, so that they bestow a certain new savor of their own. The concert must be a function of the city, the rendezvous. Place the accent firmly on New York, don't just jumble everything up together.

The singer that evening was an international celebrity. She looked so flighty, it seemed surprising that she had favored us with her presence at all, as if she could have been at any of a hundred similar celebrations. When she applied herself to the keyboard, eliciting sounds as sweet as the smoke of American cigarettes, the thought came to me that America has a sweet tooth, and there is nothing that can be done about this childish habit. But what agitated everyone even more than her singing was her fee. The fee had more power than the love songs. It proved to be the common measure uniting the diamonds on the white necks, the lavish abundance of food, the success, the tuxedos, and the talents.

The concert was arranged in a way that rendered dinner-table conversations entirely irrelevant, and everyone craned his or her neck to watch—with the exception, as always, of our Russian tables, where everyone kept half an ear on what was happening on the stage and let their bodies get on with life, pairing off with their eyes, touching knees, becoming friends and lovers in full public view. The intimate behavior of Russians at the dinner was a spectacle every bit as fascinating as a world-famous singer: the waiters were enthralled by this upsurge of erotic warmth, while the other guests, who were trying to focus on the stage, looked round at us in bewilderment and sometimes in reproach. And then, of course, the Russians rushed out to smoke, scattering ash on the steps of the rainy evening. And then the girls dashed off in coveys to the restroom to pull up their skirts and engage in candid lesbian lovemaking. For Russians the sphere of intimate relations has no rules. Everything is constructed on the multilevel metaphor of the Russian laugh, which, like a rag duster, wipes the slate clean of everything that was written on it before.

The Public Library is a building with cult status in the center of Manhattan, gray and squat with thick columns—an antiskyscraper. In the recent science-fiction film *The Day After Tomorrow*, the remnants of New York society take refuge here after the catastrophe of a global glaciation. To get warm, they burn books. We were warming ourselves, too, with old whisky in a newly revived bottle.

Finally, the parties responsible for the celebration were brought onstage—master blenders with the rosy-cheeked faces of country boys who drink three glasses of milk a day. How they ever managed to develop a taste for whisky was a mystery to me. The bagpipes began squawling with a terrible male whine, and the waiters and waitresses brought out the resurrected beverage for distribution. A good point at which to hold your breath, for if the drink was rubbish, then what was the point of this whole circus? But such laws of life do not apply to a genuinely great occasion. Even if Coca-Cola had turned up at the tables instead of whisky, the constraints of propriety and tradition would have obliged the guests in the hall to perceive it as the reborn spirit. Everybody tasted it with trepidation. And how was it? The whisky proved to be superb.

Vermeer

The guests went home in droves. Classy automobiles picked them up at the entrance and drove them off to their entirely private lives. At home they would collapse into armchairs and wearily say how tired they were.

When everyone had gone, the Russian brigade decided to start making merry. They rode the black limousines back to their downtown hotel, took off the formal suits and, wearing their "casual" jackets, dashed off in yellow taxis to a club called the Box. Outside the club there was a jostling queue of young freaks. The Russians sent their scout in through the front door, and, after no more than ten minutes, he emerged decisively from the service door and led the entire group inside. The precision of this operation indicated a knowledge of nightclub life that was truly global in scale.

The Russian brigade dissolved into the tobacco smoke with that question-mark hint of marijuana. The club's small stage presented a spectacle of mild obscenity. Some young gay guys were singing, parodying the parodists, and every now and then transvestites displayed their substantial genitalia. It was loud, and there was a smell of cheap beer. The Americans were sitting and watching the stage as if it had been the Moscow Arts Theatre.

Only, one girl suddenly jumped up off her seat, raised her sweater and showed everyone her breasts—the public was somewhat restrained in expressing its youthful delight.

It soon became boring. The Russians grabbed yellow taxis and dashed back to the hotel. They took their smartphones out of their pockets. Half an hour later some of New York's Russian girls arrived, all tall and wearing black. Tired after a humdrum day in the city, they were hungry for fun. The gathering started to buzz. Fleeting passions proved popular with all present. The New York Russian girls laughed good-naturedly at American men, whom they call "nicetomeetyous." As the girls explained, they would say hello nicely ("Nice to meet you"), spread their mouths in wide smiles, and then not know what to say for the rest of the evening.

An American is like a well (if not a deep one), while a Russian is like a river that has overflowed its banks. The Russian brigade didn't bother with cheap beer—they started tanking up on the twenty-year-old whisky that had only just been released in a limited number of bottles, a drink with which any ordinary man would merely have wetted his throat respectfully before raising his eyes heavenward to express his pleasure and delight. Consumed in large amounts, the expensive, resurrected whisky revealed itself to be an amber-yellow juice, a natural drink that had broken free of oppression by the cheap market, a beverage that had been waiting twenty-five years for the hour when it would pounce on the Russian brigade. The Moscow nightlife that was being spontaneously organized eclipsed the American special occasion. Austerity was replaced, not by absolute permissiveness, but by unpredictability. Every movement was a rejection of the American fatalism that is paradoxically called free will.

The next day I dined in the company of my American friends (including Robert Greene). It was lunch: they each ate a salad, drank a glass of wine, and tossed their credit cards into the empty breadbasket. I held out a credit card, too. They protested: I was their guest. I thanked them and went out into the city. Walking through the sunny New York that I still love today, I thought about the small, pregnant woman who had assembled our group around Cezanne's apples and suddenly felt I wanted to tell her my story. I met her and we sat drinking cappuccino in the open air in the courtyard of the Museum of Modern Art.

When I came to America for the first time, I was invited to the New York studio of Radio Liberty, and the first thing they asked me in a live interview was: "What do you like most of all about America?" I said, "Vermeer." The journalists gaped at me. They'd been expecting to hear ecstatic comments about freedom and supermarkets. "You have some wonderful paintings by Vermeer in your museums," I explained tersely. For some reason they thought I must be mocking America. When I told her this, the small pregnant woman, with her light, almost golden hair, laughed.

"And who *were* those Russians of yours?" she asked me. I shrugged and said: "Envoys of the future. . . . Well, how are things with you?" She screwed up her eyes and replied breezily: "Fine!"

A Good Monkey

Imraan Coovadia

I want to take advantage of a writer's major privilege in society, which is changing the subject, or giving an answer to a question that hasn't been asked, or, equally, posing a question when we have been asked for a statement, or constructing a list of alternatives and possibilities when somebody, with the best of intentions, demands a decision of us.

In this case my subject is the subject. It has consequences for a non-American writer who agrees to take it on as a topic. It is the kind of subject that is a difficult fit for the respondent, rather like shoes that don't fit on your feet or certain questions that put you in a difficult position ("Why do you hate me so very much?" and "Can you tell me when you began hating America ?").

The subject of this anthology—*How They See Us*—has the following consequence: it makes me one of a "them" looking as if through a window at an all of "you." But, like most writers, I have never wanted to be part of a "them"; writing privileges individual judgment and resistance to collective understandings, especially those we're supposed to have by birth or geography.

People ask, how do you feel as a Muslim? How do you

feel as an African? As a South African? Well, writers, just because we create characters, know that viewpoints are plural and contradictory and that one person, not to say one large subset of humanity, can harbor more than one feeling and that these very feelings split and mutate and won't stay still for inspection. And anyway, our feelings aren't necessarily responsible. Like Shylock's daughter Jessica, in *The Merchant of Venice*, we can be attracted by what we see through the window. We can want to join the party on the other side, and sell our mother's ring for a monkey.

In general, this position of spectatorship is a pretty miserable one, like the poor catching glimpses of the rich on the road outside an opera house. Maybe a better comparison is that it puts us in the position of the ants observing the appearing and disappearing snout of the anteater that has established itself outside our burrow. At least these ants, in my comparison, belong to the same burrow. Those of us who find ourselves on one side of our subject looking in at the other belong to a company of six-odd billion non-Americans—Uighurs, Scandinavians, Cameroonians, Kosovars.

Such company is united only by our probable grudges and unspoken envy of the scene on the other side of the telescope. But, speaking for myself at any rate, we don't want to be united by our grudges. Who, exactly, are these Kosovars and Venezuelans to me, and what could I be to them? There's a pragmatic answer to the question. In a world with one pole, our connections to each other run through America more often than not. In New York,

New Haven, and Cambridge, Massachusetts (where the new is silent), I was far more likely to meet a Venezuelan, or a Copt from Egypt, than in Cape Town where I work. In Durban, on the Indian Ocean where I grew up, foreigners are rarer than shoals of sardines.

There are symmetries that are only visible in the United States. In New York, especially in Forest Hills where I once had a place next to the disused tennis stadium, several friends were Persian Jewish and had Middle-Eastern names like Tanaze and Shireen. Their families had long organized their wills according to the Muslim formula: one share for a daughter and two shares for a son. To all intents and purposes, the Iranian Jews are culturally Muslim and religiously Jewish and from this fact I was able to figure out that I was religiously Muslim and culturally Jewish (as, I think, many writers are).

But to go back to the problem of the subject of this book: There are only two real choices open to somebody caught in this odd situation of looking over at America. They amount to submission, on the one hand, and resentment on the other. Resentment gets us to Shylock, the greatest *resentnik* on record: "Thou call'dst me dog before thou hadst a cause; / But, since I am a dog, beware my fangs."

Shylock has no center of his own. Therefore he revolves at a distance around another center, one entirely alien to him. The glamour of Christian Italy is exemplified in Belmont and its extravagant parties attended by his treacherous daughter Jessica and Lorenzo, Bassanio and Portia. Belmont is only dimly visible to Shylock.

What he glimpses of it makes him recoil.

The world of Christian partygoers seems dedicated to mockery of him in particular and Shylockism in general. "Your daughter," Tubal tells him, "spent in Genoa, as I heard, in one night fourscore ducats." A man "showed me a ring that he had of your daughter for a monkey." The ring is one that originally belonged to Shylock's late wife Leah. I have always identified, some of the way, with Jessica. Am I the only one? I would also have wanted to join the party. And I can see myself being carried away and trading that useless old ring for a good monkey.

Shylock is correctly described as a "stony adversary." He stonily opposes the very thing he orbits on the grounds that that thing instigated the conflict ("Thou call'dst me dog *before* thou hadst a cause"). Shylock is stony because he doesn't see that Venice, Belmont, Genoa have their own principles of motion, their own cares, and their own causes of celebration. Yes, they dislike Shylock but not, as he conceives it, primordially. They oppose Shylock almost without thinking, the way a club kid in LA might disapprove of Saudi Wahhabism. The contradiction is deep and irreconcilable, yet Wahhabi doctrine—and its suppression of the instincts and possibilities belonging to the nature that God, after all, gave to us—never crosses the kid's mind.

Jessica never devotes a dutiful thought to her father or mother's memory. She is, in fact, the first true teenager in world literature. Unlike her father's household (and Dubai and Saudi Arabia), Belmont and Genoa are fun.

The basic element of fun is, of course, sexual license. In our world, until very recently, America was the superpower of fun.

In *The Merchant of Venice* Portia is inhumanly Christian. She fixes Antonio's trial so that he won't have to yield a drop of his blood along with the pound of flesh. And Portia insists that Shylock convert to Christianity. Well, the old moneylender says as he departs with only half his property and none of his religion remaining, "I am content." Those three words are some of the hardest to decide about in Shakespeare. Contentment is not what we expect from Shylock, although there is just a suggestion that it comes with being a Christian. Much of the early joy of watching *The Merchant of Venice* must have come from seeing an adversary brought to this position.

I don't think it is unfair to say that, since the 1990s, America's neoconservatives have wanted the world's Muslims, from the Gaza Strip to Paris, to leave the world-historical stage mumbling the very same thing: I am content, I am content, I am content. . . .

We feel about those three words that Shakespeare expects us to believe in them yet hasn't gone to the trouble of making us believe in them. For Shakespeare, as for Belmont, Shylock is not important enough to think about. That stings. If one day the shelves of every Barnes & Noble are groaning with titles about Islam and its fatal history, the next day America has moved on. If Portia had been an American, she would have interviewed Shylock for a book of her own, *How He Sees Us*. But the next year she would have been on Oprah with another book, *The*

Quality of Mercy.

It's not just that, as we're always being told, America has a short attention span. It's that America is the most mobile society in history, perpetually demolishing and rebuilding its opinions like its cities. Almost nothing you can say about America, or assume about it, is going to be valid forever, for more than a few years, a few states, a few of the many groups composing American society. Ordered and precise language doesn't penetrate far into an ever-changing society of three hundred million, which is why Walt Whitman's favorite device is the list. Intellectuals and writers, like the ones who are writing and reading this book, overvalue the ability of words to capture the jelly of reality. It's a Shylockian habit (you *called* me a dog, Shylock reasons, and here are my *fangs*).

Writers and intellectuals aren't the only people who take words too seriously. So, it turns out, do a large number of the world's Muslims who have been turned, and turned themselves, into America's chief adversary. The affairs of the Danish cartoons and *Satanic Verses* prove that too many Muslims take words and images far too seriously, without reasoning that God also gave us the power to forget and ignore, to shut our eyes and to do something else, just as he implanted an instinct for justice in our breast. The first thing God gave us, before the scriptures and the prophets, was a common nature, and this is still the best indication of his wishes for our lives.

Anyway justice, especially justice to God, is an overvalued virtue. For God is a philosophical liberal and maybe a liberal of the Isaiah Berlin school because his commandments are irreconcilable and, most of all, he wants us to make up our minds, which he made immune to compulsion. Did George Bush call his mission in the Middle East a crusade? *Big deal.* Words come and go. A human life is made of millions of words. It's foolish to kill, even more foolish to die, for one of them.

Shylock is a literalist. He can't pass by on the side of a word. With this word "dog" they freeze him into the posture of a resenter, just as the subject "how they see us" freezes an "us" and a "them" into place. Shylock stares at the insult. It glares back at him. This interaction would be eternal except that Portia releases Shylock by imposing Christianity upon him. In this sense, which I think Shakespeare intended, Portia doesn't release Shylock from his religion so much as from the place where Venetian and European anti-Semitism put the Jews. But the world has no Portia, and no secretary-general of the United Nations can release us from our positions until forgetfulness, or some other concern, or other enmity, overtakes us.

Those of us who suffer the misfortune of being born Muslim, and not American, can find ourselves transfixed by the equivalent of the word *dog*. Whatever his faults as an intellectual historian, Edward Said was the great articulator of how doggish we feel. In *Orientalism* and afterward, Said charted all the ways in which we have been called "dog" through the centuries. Doesn't Othello boast of having murdered a Turk in Aleppo, "a circumcised dog"?

Despite their conservative detractors, Edward Said and his academic followers have no bite (although he did once throw a stone at the Israeli border wall from Lebanon). They could never say, like Shylock, "*beware my fangs.*" Said's key insight is about what it is like to live in a world where what is said is said by someone else about oneself. If *Orientalism*, in 1979, was nominally about how *they* (the Europeans) see *us* (Muslims, Arabs, Indians), its actual subject was our postmodern world of television and now electronic communications.

Astronomers worry about how an alien civilization would reckon with the broadcasts it picks up from planet Earth: what would they make of *Baywatch*, *Survivor*, *24*? How would they envisage a relationship with humanity after watching *Independence Day* or *Alien 3*?

Well, those of us who aren't American have been running this experiment throughout the twentieth century. We live in a globe of American radiations, American trends, American brands and thoughts. We overhear America all the time, eavesdrop on American life and American perspectives on ourselves in the way Shylock eavesdrops on Belmont, Venice, and Genoa in all the pain of his exclusion. Electronic America winds its way into our fantasies and makes Jessicas of each and every one of us. If we overreact to America, it's because America is already a splinter in our flesh. Just because America is the land of mobility and discontent, of the "pursuit of happiness" and not its promise, doesn't mean it's effective at governing the world. Legitimacy means getting others to say, "I am content," or "I've had enough; I give up." But where is that message in Walt Whitman, undisciplined, promiscuous, and voracious for everything? Whitman says: "I celebrate myself, and sing myself, / And what I assume you shall assume, / For every atom belonging to me as good belongs to you."

And what if the Shia in Iraq or the Tutsi in Rwanda don't assume what Walt Whitman assumes? What if they are in love with their own assumptions, their own histories and starting places? What if they don't see what Hamlet and Whitman see—that "every atom belonging to me" has once belonged to somebody else and will belong to yet another in the future? How far can a love of humanity penetrate against human beings who don't love humanity but only their subsections of it? And how about those who don't love at all but seek their own idea of heavenly justice? Shakespeare gives Shylock a more stubborn sense of human intractability. Explaining his own waywardness, Shylock observes:

> *Some men there are, love not a gaping pig;*
> *Some, that are mad if they behold a cat;*
> *And others, when the bagpipe sings i' the nose,*
> *Cannot contain their urine: for affection,*
> *Mistress of passion, sways it to the mood*
> *Of what it likes or loathes.*

Whitmanian universalism may be the Declaration of Independence set in poetic lines, but its boundaries are not those of humanity itself but those of the United States. In Whitman's America, the "nation of nations," which has absorbed more diversity than any state on earth, one hears always of Americans and never of human beings and the general interest of humanity.

As for the neoconservatives who have sailed the American ship of state up the creek, imaginative writers—who want to create characters with their own freedom of motion and their own conflicting perspectives—have long understood what their problem is. It wasn't merely hubris at work, or the need for an American president to do something great with his term in office. The neoconservatives and their Rumsfeldian and Cheneyite allies made a basic mistake about human complexity and agency. Portia can make Shylock say, "I am content," but only at the cost of our belief in Shakespeare at that moment.

In her 1866 novel *Felix Holt*, George Eliot borrows an image from Adam Smith (ultimately from medieval political thought):

> Fancy what a game at chess would be if all the chessmen had passions and intellects, more or less small and cunning: if you were not only uncertain about your adversary's men, but a little uncertain also about your own; if your knight could shuffle himself on to a new square by the sly; if your bishop, in disgust at your castling, could wheedle your pawns out of their places; and if your pawns, hating you because they are pawns, could make away from their appointed posts that you might get checkmate on a sudden.[...] You might be the longest-headed of deductive reasoners, and yet you might be beaten by your own pawns. You would be especially likely to be beaten, if you depended arrogantly on your mathematical imagination, and regarded your passionate pieces with contempt.

George Eliot, like Smith, concludes that "this imaginary chess is easy compared with the game a man has to play against his fellow-men with other fellow-men for his instruments."

There couldn't be a nicer summary of what's gone wrong between the world and America since the 1990s. Some of it is your fault. Some of it is our fault (for existing). And a lot of it, especially in the Middle East, is a result of the basic waywardness of human chessmen—"pawns, hating you because they are pawns" is a brief version of what political scientists call geopolitical balancing—combined with the contempt inherent in the far right wing, and far left, view of history.

Of course the United States Constitution is the greatest political expression of this doubt about the controllability of human beings. The breakdown between America and the rest of us is only going to be fixed when America again falls under the spell of what Abraham Lincoln called its better angels. Those better angels, unlike Portia, know that we're no angels and that, in fact, there are no angels and there is no way of the angels. We're Jessicas and Shylocks. Some of us "love not a gaping pig." Some of us "are mad [to] behold a cat." And, as Shylock knew, "others, when the bagpipe sings i' the nose, / Cannot contain their urine."

Fiddlers and Failures

Terry Eagleton

The story is told in Ireland of a fiddlers' competition out in the wilds of the west, the winner of which would become all-Ireland champion. (The title "all-Ireland champion" is admittedly a little loose: one bumps into scores of such uniquely titled fiddlers up and down the country, as though every second woman on the street were to turn out to be Miss Arkansas.) The first competitor for the award stepped up to the front: a svelte, distinguished, silver-haired gentleman bedecked in evening dress, exquisitely coiffed and bearing in his hand—no less—a Stradivarius. Resting the instrument against his chin with a confident flourish, he drew the bow vigorously across the strings and began to play.

And by God he was useless.

The second candidate for stardom then turned to face the audience—a slick-haired, shining-toothed, slightly flashy type in a well-tailored gray suit, carrying in his hand an expensive but not classic violin. With an ingratiating bow, he placed the instrument under his chin and began to play.

And by God he was useless.

The judges were just on the point of declaring a no-winner when there was a commotion at the back of the

room. Despite some evident reluctance, a third competitor was being forced to the front by his friends—a
tiny, shrunken, octogenarian fellow in a crumpled old
suit buttoned up with bits of string and hardly a scrap of
seat to his trousers. In his withered claw lay a fiddle as
decrepit as himself, its strings frayed and peeling, its body
held together by elastic bands. Shrinking from the crowd,
but urged on by his loyal colleagues, he placed the fiddle
beneath his chin with a quivering hand and softly drew
the tattered bow across it.

And by God he was useless, too.

I take it that this is among other things a deeply un-
American story. Indeed, the Irish are in general deeply
un-American, despite their long historical entanglement
with the country—as opposed to the British, who are in
general not un-American but anti-American. In the late
century, whole villages in the west of Ireland were kept
afloat by the New York Police Department, whose Irish
officers would send remittances home. The so-called
"special relationship" is not with Britain but with Ireland.
It is the Irish, not the British, who do not require visas to
enter the United States.

One of the key differences between the British and the
Irish is that the latter tend to be fond of Americans while
the former, by and large, are not. In one sense, this is
scarcely a cause for surprise, since where would the Micks
be without the Yanks? As one Dublin wag commented,
when Saint Patrick drove the snakes out of Ireland,
they took refuge in Chicago City Hall. This affection,
however, is bemusing to an Englishman of Irish prov-

enance like myself who has long lived in Ireland, since it is hard—at least in terms of *sensibility*—to think of two more dissimilar nations. The fiddler joke is un-American to my own ears partly because it mischievously pulls the rug out from under a dewy-eyed sentimentalism that has more than a smack of the States about it. Americans in general are more sentimental than Europeans, which is part of their general tendency to wear their spiritual innards on their sleeves. It is also the case that a hardheaded, brusquely pragmatic society, where what mostly counts is money, is likely to be sentimental simply because sentimentality is the only poor parody of genuine feeling such pragmatism is able to muster. The Irish exist for other people to be sentimental about, but they are a profoundly unsentimental, unromantic people themselves—a fact that is hardly surprising, given their catastrophic history. (I assume, incidentally, that generalizations about nations or ethnic groups are perfectly acceptable, however nervous liberals may feel about them. For a materialist, it would be astonishing if a group of people had shared roughly the same conditions over a considerable period of time without developing some psychological traits in common.)

Like a good deal of Irish humor, the fiddler fable works by upending or inverting emotional commonplaces. As with the wit of Oscar Wilde, it is nothing if not perverse, taking some (usually English) piece of conventional wisdom and flipping it inside out, standing it on its head, turning it back to front. Sexuality was one of Wilde's least interesting perversities. His wit represents an anti-

colonial smack at English conceptual and linguistic assur-
ances, a gleeful delight in debunking and deflating, which
in Irish culture stretches all the way from Jonathan Swift
to Samuel Beckett. The fiddler story maliciously baffles
conventional narrative expectations, depriving us of our
roseate Hollywood ending. Like much Irish humor, it is
latently aggressive, the wit of those with a secret grudge
against the self-satisfied, smoothly predictable certainties
of the established order; and in this the Irish resemble
not Americans as a whole, whose humor is far heartier
and blander, but New York Jews. It is not mysterious
that the protagonist of the greatest Irish novel ever written bears the name of Bloom.

The fiddler joke works by bathos, building up high-
minded assumptions about the virtuous poor only glee-
fully to puncture them; and bathos is by far the most
common trope in Irish literature. Hacking the world
savagely down to size is a distinctively Irish pursuit.
Distinctive, though not peculiar, since it is shared to some
extent by the British. Americans, by contrast, always seem
to us Europeans to be inflating things rather than deflating them. There is a chronic over-the-topness about the
nation. Sending twenty flashing, screeching police cars
to arrest someone found smoking a joint might serve as
an example. American prison sentences, fruit of a brutally
puritan punitiveness, appear grossly inflated in our spine-
lessly liberal view. The United States is the land of hubris
and hyperbole. It cannot just give up smoking or stop eating so much but must make an almighty fuss about it. (My
own rather eccentric theory of the American obsession

with (non-)smoking is that smoke acts as a contaminating connection between one's own body and someone else's, in a country with so much space that an American will murmur "Excuse me" if he or she comes within ten yards of you. It doesn't happen in Beijing.).

As far as hyperbole goes, the nation also resounds with a solemn, sententious, mid-Victorian, hideously earnest public rhetoric, which to our ears sounds merely embarrassing. No British politician could refer to God or This Great Country of Ours without provoking an incredulous jeer. Americans seem to us either racily idiomatic or ponderously rhetorical. There is a quality of innocence about this hand-on-heart discourse that makes Europeans feel soiled and jaded. No English or Irish person would say something like "I appreciate your patience and understanding, sir, and will make a commitment to you," as a Duke student once said to me. They would simply suspect you were making fun of them. Freud once remarked that the average individual is both far less moral than he suspected, and far more moral as well; and of few human beings is this truer than Americans. If only they would stop being so portentously, self-consciously Moral, they might prove to be better people. American children's TV programs, for example, are extraordinarily didactic compared to British ones, as though play is useless unless a civic moral can be instantly extracted from it. Moral earnestness in Britain is for shopkeepers, not for the kind of patrician whom many of the English would secretly love to be. The trick is to be languid and off-hand in a stylish sort of way, not pathetically puffed up with your own petty-bourgeois sincerity. When someone thanks you, you reply "Not at all" or "Don't mention it" rather than "It's my pleasure" or "You're very welcome."

The English are would-be Cavaliers, and look down on their American cousins as unreconstructed Roundheads. If there is a cult of irony in Britain, it is among other things because truth, too, is for the lower middle classes. Truth is boring and petty-bourgeois, whereas irony is playful, inessential, and hence aristocratic. Aristocrats don't need the truth because they have enough money to insulate them against its more rebarbative implications. As a regular contributor to the British *Guardian* newspaper, I was dumbfounded to be told by a *New York Times* journalist who was interviewing me for that newspaper that I was forbidden to use irony. I couldn't have been more astonished if she had told me that *New York Times* journalists were expected to garnish their reports with a liberal sprinkling of the most scabrous expletives they could muster. Americans tend to admire plain speaking, which is part of their puritan heritage, whereas some of the English, and certainly some of the Irish, tend to regard plain speaking as a disability for which a course of therapy might be required. Why use only four words where forty would do? Some Americans seem to regard metaphorical lushness in fiction as "effete," whereas an excessive repetition of the copula figures as a sign of virile authenticity ("and then he hit me in the jaw and I fell over and there was blood everywhere and he was still grinning that goddam stupid grin and . . . ").

There are other forms of hyperbole as well. Nervous

of all vulgar self-vaunting, the average Irish or English parent would never drive a vehicle sporting the sign "My Child is on the Honor Roll." You might just see a satirical sign reading "My Child is a Serial Killer," but certainly nothing as innocently self-affirmative as one occasionally sees in the States. Praising one's children in public is a practice distasteful to most Europeans. The Irish in particular are masters at putting themselves down, in case others do it for them. In small nations like Ireland, Belgium, or Norway, where everyone was at school with everyone else, you know each other too well to be impressed by each other's achievements, and standing out from the crowd is in any case deeply inadvisable. In such thinly populated communities, envy is the only human force stronger than sex, so that claiming some kind of individual distinctiveness is spurned as profoundly antisocial. This can make for an oppressively claustrophobic climate. In the USA, by contrast, the habit seems to be to puff yourself up. Few nations appear so ruthlessly goal-oriented and noisily self-assertive. No other people to my knowledge uses the word "aggressive" as a compliment, and no other group of human beings apart from psychoanalysts speaks so repetitively of "dreams." In a curious collective narcissism, Americans also use the word "America," at least in their public discourse, far more than the Malays speak of Malaysia or Bulgarians speak of Bulgaria. The word signifies a value as well as a fact, an aspiration as well as a description, which is not the case with "Paraguay." All this self-asserting does not come across to most Europeans as mere stereotypical

American boasting, since they understand that a cultural habit is at stake here. To some extent, it is one redeemed precisely by its wide-eyed innocence of the fact that it sounds so unpleasant. It has, however, a covert affinity with less acceptable kinds of hubris and hyperbole, like those which sent the United States into Iraq, so that to this extent its naïveté cannot entirely salvage it.

To listen to some Americans talk, one would think that world history held no tragedy as stark as that of the destruction of the World Trade Center; whereas the truth is that exactly three decades earlier, the United States violently overthrew the democratically elected government of Chile and installed in its place an odious dictator who with U.S. connivance went on to murder far more innocents than ever died in the horror of 9/11. The country also armed and championed an autocrat in Indonesia who almost certainly disposed of more blameless lives than did Saddam Hussein. In its time, Europe has committed atrocities to equal or exceed these massacres; but the difference is that Europeans do not particularly regard themselves as good guys in the way that some Americans tend to do. They are far too cynical for that, which is one reason why they are not exactly good guys; but they are also commendably realistic not to perceive themselves as such. It is a familiar truth, however, that a belief in an absolute opposition between good guys and bad guys belongs to America's puritan heritage, which is no doubt one reason why Jacques Derrida's style of deconstruction was so eagerly embraced by frustrated radical academics. When in doubt, the English think of a pendulum that swings to and fro between extreme positions. A certain relaxed tolerance, a dim sense of the mixedness of things ("It takes all kinds to make a world"; "There's good and bad in all of us"; "It'd be a funny world if we all thought the same") is part of their routine discourse. This does not mean that they are paragons of liberal virtue. On the contrary, many of them would feel thoroughly at home wearing pointed white hoods. But a suspicion of stark extremes is built into the way they know they are supposed to think, and sometimes even do think.

The astonishing voluntarism of much American ideology—the belief that you can crack it if you try, that the sky's the limit, that the word "can't" is almost as offensive as the term "Communist" has a grossly naïve ring in the ears of a continent buried beneath the historical detritus of centuries. There is a deeply destructive quality about this cult of the naked, unhoused, muscle-bound will, which can end up burning the bodies of Arab children. Like all desire, it is virulently antimaterialist. It fails to grasp that constraints are constitutive of our species-being, not simply obstacles to be surmounted. If the United States indeed ends up annihilating the planet, it will be its crazed idealism, not its crude materialism, that will be to blame. It does not seem to have learnt the Freudian lesson that the chronically idealizing superego is as much a source of destruction and despair as a well-spring of vision and exaltation. Ideals tend sadistically to rub your nose in your own ineluctable failure. Once they get out of hand, they can become terroristic. Not seeing this is a large part of what Europeans mean by American innocence. Modernity has witnessed a form of discourse that devotes itself to investigating the mechanisms by which the resplendent revolutionary ideals of the middle class, to which the United States rightly pays such homage, tend to twist into their opposite whenever one attempts to put them into practice. This discourse, however, is known as Marxism and is not the most popular idiom in Grand Rapids, Michigan. On the other hand, Americans who speak of money as "the bottom line" are unwitting adherents of Marx's doctrine of base and superstructure.

The Faustian myth of the American dream, that pernicious fantasy that has damaged and befuddled the lives of so many decent men and women, must accordingly be countered by the idea of tragedy. I mean by the idea of tragedy the recognition that only those communities or individuals that maintain a secret compact with failure have a hope of flourishing. The writing of Samuel Beckett is a case in point. It is not in the least irrelevant to this fact that Beckett was Irish. (Indeed, when he was asked by a rather callow French journalist whether he was English, he properly replied "*Au contraire.*") A suffering solidarity with breakdown, loss, and futility, so the great tragic artists and thinkers have always insisted, is the vital precondition for any achievement that will not eventually crumble to dust in your hands. Psychoanalysis understands this tragic doctrine in its own way, as does the Christian faith, which in the United States has for the most part been blasphemously pressed into the service of what D. H. Lawrence called the bitch-goddess Success. It is not the case in the USA, as it is not the case in Europe, that you will recognize Yahweh for who he is when you see the hungry being filled with good things and the rich being sent empty away.

The United States, however, is a profoundly antitragic society, even if it is now living through one of the most tragic phases of its history. You cannot really flourish if you hate a loser. As in the finest tragic art, it is only by recognizing your own distorted visage in the scum and refuse of the earth, discerning in the monstrous terror at your gates a thing of darkness that you must acknowledge as your own, that you have the faintest hope of salvation. American politicians' talk of hope (a key American term, like *comfortable with, reach out to, awesome,* and *stay focused*) is intended to bypass this unutterably painful process of self-disinvestment, not burrow all the way through it in the wan faith that you might emerge somewhere on the other side. This is why all such talk of hope, change, morning in America, and bravely facing the future is as bogus as talk of world peace in the face of the squalid concentration camp that is the Gaza strip.

If one would wish the United States a touch more reticence and obliquity (as well as that it should start using the rather beautiful word *children* in place of the ugly monosyllable *kids*), one would also wish it to acknowledge what Hegel once called the power of the negative. In a square-jawed, self-affirmative culture, speaking negatively about something begins to sound like a thought crime. "How was your holiday?" an American asks. "Perfectly dreadful," you truthfully reply, watching the faint flicker of puzzlement and discomfort in his eyes. Wherever possible, you are expected to be upbeat. The American word for an unmitigated disaster is *challenge*. Failure is scarcely to be admitted. Even cemeteries are to be spoken of as places where a good deal of activity goes on (jogging, flower-tending, and the like), not as dumping grounds for the dead. A mistrust of the negative is one reason why there is so dismally little satire in the country, if one discounts the unmatchable *Simpsons*. Negativity is mistaken for nihilism, and nihilism is bad for ideological morale. This is why rival political commentators arguing the toss on television must keep smiling and joshing, to assure the viewer that there is no *real* conflict here. There is, after all, only one political party in this supposed democracy: the capitalist party. Such compulsory joshing and grinning also serves to confirm that these individuals are *human*, given the quaint U.S. assumption that there is something sinisterly robotic about discussing ideas without an occasional sob, chuckle, "Look-it" or "There ya go again."

There are many reasons, then, why not to live in the United States—one of the most pressing of all being that its inhabitants rise and retire ridiculously early. In this, too, the puritan lineage can be gleaned, along with the proddings of the profit motive. No civilized society would require one to rise before 10 a.m., or to retire before midnight. Predawn power-breakfasts are quite as barbaric as throwing Christians to the lions. Some Americans, as aghast at such incivilities as any European observer, have fled the country, taken up home in Naples or Marrakesh or Copenhagen, and embarked there on the painful process of de-Americanization. Such cities these days are thronged with recovering Americans, all of them at various stages of the twelve-step program of AA. Yet there are several good reasons to live in the place as well. And in case this statement, after all this carping and criticizing, might sound mildly implausible, let me confess that some of my best friends are Americans. My wife, for example, along with two of my children. It is true that my eldest American child could scarcely be described as a fanatical patriot, having rashly attempted to scale the spiked railings of the U.S. embassy in Dublin during an anti-Iraq-war demonstration shouting obscenities rarely heard in the mouth of a nine-year-old.

Even so, few countries of my acquaintance manifest such a robust civic consciousness as the United States. The Irish have traditionally displayed very little such civic sense, largely because the country for several centuries was not their own. There is a covert connection between British imperialism and all that shocking saliva on the streets of Dublin. Laws are not matters that the Irish obey in too slavish or literal a spirit, even today, since many such laws traditionally worked to their detriment. The British have little civic spirit largely because of the admirable stubbornness or "bloody-mindedness" of the traditional British working class, who were never fooled into believing that the country was their own in the same sense that it belonged to Winston Churchill, and who unlike many American workers would never dream of speaking of "our" business or company. Whereas

American workers and entrepreneurs tend to reveal a bright-eyed "can-do" attitude, the stereotypical British worker will stand for ten minutes before whatever is to be fixed shaking his head disconsolately and will only by gradual degrees be drawn into a grudging admission that it is not hopelessly beyond repair. Outsiders who are not familiar with this ritual, and not prepared to collaborate conscientiously in its every baroque move, will be left with leaky pipes or blown fuses.

The United States, by contrast, has kept alive something of the sense of civic fellowship and social responsibility that inspired its revolutionary origins. No doubt it needs to, as a counterweight to the divisive effects of both multiculturalism and capitalist individualism. Even so, there are few peoples as pleasant and courteous to one another as Americans. By and large, the Chinese treat one another with notable roughness, whereas we English prefer not to encounter one another at all. If we can get away with a phone call or a coy note rather than a face-to-face meeting, we will most certainly do so. The English regard human contact as greatly overrated, not least by the Americans. By and large, they tend to believe that once you have seen one specimen of humanity you have seen the lot. Americans believe in individualism, while the English believe in that very different phenomenon, idiosyncrasy. And idiosyncrasy is among other things a way of keeping others at arm's length. It is an acceptably flamboyant form of unsociability. There are Oxbridge dons who would wish to be remembered not for their pathbreaking history of Byzantium, but for the fact that they frequented a pub every night with a loquacious parrot perched on their shoulder. On the whole, individualism in the United States belongs to the economic realm, while culture is largely a matter of conformity. In Britain, culture is among other things the domain of individual idiosyncrasy, while too brash an entrepreneurialism still tends to be frowned on.

Idiosyncrasy is an extravagant form of privacy, a kind of taking shelter from others in the depths of oneself; and it is this privacy that Europeans tend to find so absent in the USA. Not, to be sure, that there is any lack of gated communities or "Keep Out" notices in the place. The country is more thickly plastered with stern public prohibitions than any I know. What bemuses Europeans is the apparent assumption (again puritan in provenance) that what is not instantly externalized or articulated does not truly exist. It is this that some Europeans tend to mistake for a lack of human depth or interiority. It is not that there are no depths, but that the depths are more on the surface than they are in Zurich or Zagreb. The Irish, by contrast, can appear easy and spontaneous, but have long nurtured (partly for political reasons) a complex culture of secrecy, and are much less instantly decipherable than they appear. If the British and the Americans are divided by the same language, in Bernard Shaw's immortal phase, it is partly because the last thing the British believe is that what you see is what you get.

The United States and Latin America: Inevitable Nostalgia

Fernando Báez
Translated by Kristina Cordero

I.

The first time I ever heard anyone utter the words "United States" was in San Félix, the town where I was born. I was four or five years old at the time and lived in dignified poverty, the sole advantage of which was the absolute freedom I was given to learn to read without a care in the world. My village was an impoverished little hamlet situated along the broad banks of the magnificent Orinoco River, which, from the sixteenth century onward, had served as a port of entry and departure for the hulking ships that greedily divested the region of Guayana, in Venezuela, of the gold that pirate Walter Raleigh so extolled. Later on it would become the unyielding axis of the sloops, schooners, and steamships that boldly extracted iron and precious stones as well as the tanned hides of ferocious tigers, endless anacondas, treacherous alligators, and fossils that evoked a world that was already hopelessly lost.

My mind wanders back, in that time outside of time,

to the day my father, an honest—that is, unemployed—lawyer, gave me a gift. With a pomp and circumstance I will never forget, his eyes beaming with generosity, he handed me a light-green volume with golden lettering. It was a biography, he said, of the politician he most admired in the world: John Fitzgerald Kennedy. At my father's side, wearing a hat that clung to his head, a blue-striped shirt, and black silk pants, stood a man whose name I have since forgotten—in fact I only recently learned that he had been one of the few consultants to survive the nationalization of the old Iron Mines Company, a supplier of the Fairless Works plant that belonged to U.S. Steel, in the state of Pennsylvania. In my presence, the two men spoke a language that was foreign to me. Much later that night, or perhaps it was already early morning by then, when I saw that my father was once again alone, attempting to read the previous day's newspaper, I asked him where his friend was from, for I was intrigued and somewhat astonished by his red coloring. My father dryly responded: the United States. That was all he said—I don't know if he intended to say anything else, but in any case those two words were plenty.

A week or two later, I decided that I had to learn more about that enigmatic country and went to the public library, where I enjoyed the discreet aid of an aunt by marriage, a widow who had been the straitlaced supervisor of the place for several years. The library was little more than a blue house with a flat oak roof held up by a number of ancient tree trunks that rather incongruously held various thin sheets of zinc in place. The inside

was dominated by broken shelving and brand-new book-
cases, barely illuminated by the scant light that came
through the windows, making the collections seem scat-
tered, dispersed. The rooms were either locked up with
a key that had disappeared quite unapologetically, or else
left open to reveal spaces that had become storage areas
for the pamphlets of the political parties of the moment.
Nothing was where it was supposed to be. Quite often,
my aunt would place in my hands the most dazzling
illustrated volumes; they filled me with emotion. Luck
was on my side when, after telling her about my father's
friend, she pulled out a heavy dictionary with color plates
and showed me a map of the United States, a map of
Kansas, photos of canyons in Colorado, drawings that
unsuccessfully portrayed colonists from the *Mayflower*,
Edison's light bulb, Franklin's lightning rod, the faces of
Martin Luther King and Elvis Presley, a New York sky-
scraper and an out-of-focus photograph of an astronaut
walking on the moon. Before I knew it the hours had
slipped away, smoothly, rapidly. As if the rest of the world
had disappeared.

It goes without saying, of course, that I went home
and declared to my mother, a long-suffering Spanish
woman, that I, too, could become an astronaut. Anyone
who could have seen me right then, with my torn pants,
mended shirt, and unconventional hairstyle sculpted
by the pillow I slept on rather than the comb I did not
possess, would have laughed out loud. But I fervently
believed what I said. And I believed the things I read in
books: I could cry while staring at an etching of a dying

Don Quixote and I cut up pieces of paper to create the rocket in which I would finally set out to explore the farthest recesses of outer space. With Manuel, my childhood playmate, I made a prototype for a wooden ship that we launched in the river and would have drowned in had it not been for the providential hand of one of those lone fishermen who spend days on end in search of the perfect fish that never materializes from the water's depths.

Without many other distractions, apart from those of plunging into rivers or playing hide-and-seek, I was quite taken by the local movie theater that an Italian businessman by the name of Marconi opened in our village. It lasted only two weeks before going bankrupt, but before it did, I managed to see a film that changed my life. During this time when I still didn't have a clear picture of the United States, I was at least able to imagine it thanks to *The Wizard of Oz* featuring Judy Garland, an unparalleled experience for me even though I didn't understand much of it. But how could I not delight in the wise scarecrow and the frightened lion? How could I not realize that this was a new way of looking at the world, through the lens of fantasy and enchantment? American movies had already left their mark on the planet, and soon they cast a hypnotic spell on me that has dissipated only recently, though leaving behind intense aftereffects redolent of Chaplin, Welles, and Hitchcock.

The man whom my friends, between giggles, called "the gringo" returned to my house on more than a few occasions. The routine of his visits was always the same, as if copied from a manual on survival in the tropics. He would bring two beers, a pipe that he would never smoke, and four or five bags of peanuts. Once settled into the house's one rocking chair—the same one my grandmother sat in as she swore never to forgive my grandfather for his infidelities—he would begin to talk, and though I, of course, did not understand him, his words consoled my father and made him laugh in the middle of all the hardships we lived with. They would also argue sometimes, suddenly falling silent as if they had run out of words, the obstinacy of their convictions giving way to the longest of silences. Occasionally they would exchange books, and I recall their speaking about Rómulo Gallegos and William Faulkner—I imagine they were talking about the time the two men met in Caracas, a powerful encounter that brought together two literary traditions born from the telluric forces of the American continent. Never again would a meeting of this sort between two literary giants come to pass as it did in the 1960s.

Seated next to my father, who suffered from a most invincible gloom, I was able to appreciate the value of argument. For it was during one of these discussions with his American friend that an inconceivable debate was sparked by a strange word that I would come to understand only later on, in my adolescence: Vietnam. I remember how the man, upon hearing that fatal word, sprang from his chair, tense, jumping up to spit out a few words before finally surrendering to the evidence as my father gazed at him with a perfectly serene countenance. After that, the word became a taboo, and suddenly it became terribly difficult to return to the original idea that had set them off on their path of sharing unexpected, revelatory moments. The man was finally bid farewell one December 31st, without explanations, at a rather unusual hour of the day, and only after several long weeks had gone by did I learn that he had returned to his home city with a heavy heart, because by then he considered himself an honorary Venezuelan.

II.

Despite my attempt at re-creating a sense of those pleasant times, I am left with only vague, half-explored recollections, and the uncomfortable feeling that my father, who died of Parkinson's disease not long ago, bequeathed to me—either knowingly or not—a memory of and a commitment to friendship, but most of all to dialogue and cultural exchange. My particular image of the United States, until I was almost twenty years old, was an orthodox inheritance. Incredible as it may seem, in my house, books like Eduardo Galeano's *The Open Veins of Latin America* or Noam Chomsky's *The Responsibility of Intellectuals* were not read, nor were the works of Mario Benedetti, Augusto Roa Bastos, Pablo Neruda, or Vladimir Ilich Lenin. Abundant attention, however, was paid to the works of Ernest Hemingway, Ray Bradbury, Francis Scott Fitzgerald, Raymond Chandler, Walt Whitman, Henry James, Washington Irving, Isaac Asimov, and Jack Kerouac. When I began to write, at the age of twelve or thirteen, I was enthralled by Edgar Allan Poe. At my father's behest I memorized the poem "The Raven" and repeated its verses over and over again.

The most lukewarm cold war in history played itself out in my home, in its own idiosyncratic way, with no pressure, because my father refused to allow us to buy anything by Karl Marx or Friedrich Engels. At the university, I was ordered to keep away from all manner of anti-imperialist student protests, conferences, concerts, or poetry readings, and I regarded all leftist initiatives with suspicion. The one and only time I ever mentioned, in the softest voice I could manage, that Ché Guevara—and his murder—had caught my attention, my mother dissolved in tears. The harshest criticism I ever heard—and ever will hear, I am sure—was prompted by the supposed heresy that fell from my lips, and that was how I came to realize that my family's vision of things was firmly anchored in the Kennedy era, in speeches of the "I have a dream" variety, at a time when it seemed that the United States could look forward to a friendly future with the popular Latin American sectors. This was also the time when the Alliance for Progress was inaugurated, a moment in which sustained, efficient social development seemed possible. Kennedy was the leader who had said: "If a free society cannot help the many who are poor, it cannot save the few who are rich."

I speak of these things, personal as they are, because they are an integral part of how and why I came to admire the United States—how could I not? Today, however, I can only feel deeply saddened when I think of how irrevocably that optimism—so fresh, so genuine—has been lost, transformed into the growing skepticism that, at the present moment, precludes me from believing in the benevolence of the most recent actions undertaken by the country that the historian Samuel P. Huntington defines quite aptly as the lonely superpower. I don't believe the United States has ever been quite as alone and menaced by danger as it is now.

In my own case, without a doubt, two or three factors in particular contributed to the erosion of my faith. One of them, the most sinister, infamous, and incomprehensible of them all, was the unconscionable tacit support that the administration of Richard M. Nixon lent the coup d'etat perpetrated by General Augusto Pinochet on September 11, 1973, in Chile, that led to the death of the country's president, Salvador Allende. In my home this produced conflicts, insignificant at first and more serious over time, that never culminated in much of anything but that undermined certain time-honored family understandings. Often I would argue about the damage wrought by Henry Kissinger, the Nobel Peace Prize laureate most frequently associated with wars, who encouraged so many ruthless military officers to stage coups, commit genocide, and inflict torture, all in the name of keeping the region free from "Cubanization."

It was terrible to experience so intensely the implementation of the thesis of the ideological war in Latin America. Countless writers and editors were assassinated or silenced; millions of men and women disappeared or were forced into exile. During the 1970s and 1980s, the officers of the U.S. Department of State seemed to be convinced that all evil was preferable to the expansion of the left, which, no doubt, took advantage of mistakes made on the economic, social, and cultural fronts. One miscalculation after another, attempts were made to build relationships based on amnesia, on indirect and bloody intervention. By a certain point, so many negative elements had conspired to destroy my image of the United States that I finally ran out of arguments with which to defend the respect I had previously felt for so long. What finally shattered inside me was something of a moral nature, and it feels no more whole now whenever I think back and wonder how it was possible to support murderers like Alfredo Stroessner, who governed Paraguay from 1954 to 1989 with utmost cruelty (and tried to make Paraguay a haven for Nazi fugitives).

Another deplorable fact that dampened my enthusiasm for the United States was the direct participation of its intelligence agencies in the Central American conflict during the days of Daniel Ortega's Sandinista government. A number of Ronald Reagan's advisers believed the Nicaraguan movement to be a direct and imminent danger, and they decided to train, arm, and finance Sandinista opponents, sponsoring a civil war that left thirty-eight thousand people dead and seventeen billion dollars in losses. This situation repeated itself in El Salvador and most poignantly in Guatemala, where two hundred thousand people died as the result of thirty-six years of conflicts between the armed forces and guerrilla movements. Hard as it is for me to believe, the person who made me take note of all this was the American intellectual Noam Chomsky, who ultimately became central to my way of thinking. I have Chomsky to thank, not only for helping me see that as an intellectual I have a responsibility to denounce situations in which human rights are being disregarded, but also for helping me to recover my faith in the possibility of fighting, from a non-Marxist perspective, the misguided foreign policy of several U.S. administrations.

The United States has intervened, on 150 separate occasions, in a considerable portion of the twenty-two million square kilometers that comprise Latin America, leaving its catastrophic, painful mark on countries like Haiti, the Dominican Republic, Grenada, Brazil, Bolivia, and Peru. Instead of contributing to the region through humanitarian missions, the U.S. government opted instead to step up its military presence. Today, some two thousand active members of the United States armed forces are deployed in the region, which includes the Caribbean. SOCSOUTH (Special Operations Command South), created in 1947, is responsible for all the activities of the so-called Southern Command, which has bases in Soto Cano, Honduras; Panama; Comalapa, El Salvador; Liberia, Costa Rica; Reina Beatriz, on the island of Aruba; Hato, on the island of Curaçao; Vieques, Puerto Rico; Jamaica; Iquitos, Santa Lucía; and Nanay, in Peru; Tres Esquinas (air base), Larandia, Puerto Leguizamó, and Leticia, in Colombia; Chaparé, Bolivia; and I cannot help but conclude by mentioning Guantánamo, which has become a symbol for horror much as the gulags were in the now-extinct Soviet Union. When I was a little boy in Venezuela, we had medical doctors, engineers, businessmen, members of humanitarian missions, singers— all of them from the United States. And then, somehow, all of a sudden, they were replaced with soldiers.

Things happened so fast, I don't think anyone understood how. On the stifling day of September 11, 2001, a group of suicidal Arab militants belonging to the organization known as Al Qaeda hijacked four airplanes and attacked the United States. Their trail of destruction extended from the World Trade Center in New York all the way to an entire wing of the Pentagon. I remember I was eating at the home of friends. Someone turned on the television set and despite the terrible reception we watched as columns of smoke came billowing out from a massive tower. And then, it must have been a few minutes later, a passenger plane dove into a building and thousands of papers went flying into the air. Debilitated beyond measure, the structure was unable to withstand the heat and collapsed, something I had thought impossible. Not since Pearl Harbor had the United States been attacked on its own territory by enemy forces. Like so many other people, I could not help crying, and my rage was not long in coming. I knew something terrible was about to happen.

Destiny is what it is, but more often than not a cataclysmic event has a way of redirecting our paths. And because I want to tell the story of how my skepticism came about, I ought to explain how, following the Iraq invasion in 2003, I received an invitation to be part of an international commission charged with investigating the matter of the libraries, archives, and museums destroyed in the wake of Saddam Hussein's demise. For the past ten years I have been gathering information about cultural destruction, and recently I finished what may be the only book-length work on the topic—yet that trip to Iraq was the only thing capable of giving me back the measure of doubt I needed to fully abandon the myth of the United States as a nation capable of contributing to peace.

Panic always seems to be out there somewhere, ready to strike without a moment's notice. That was how I felt while standing in the National Library of Baghdad (Al Maktaba Al Wataniya), in Rasaf, where the Defense Ministry is located. The National Library lost almost a million books. After spending some time there, I went to the Archaeological Museum where more than twenty-five thousand pieces were pillaged and then sold on the black market. I found myself standing before a majestic, elongated structure, the façade of which was flanked by towers on either side, a building the color of sand that was being guarded by a tank with a cannon that had the words "Greetings from the United States of America" written on its side. Quite the paradox. I now know that all the libraries and museums of Iraq were torn to pieces, and that the United States may have caused as many as one million deaths in the country. The worst thing of all, however, is that the miserable Bush administration destroyed the legitimacy of the war against terror by using false evidence to justify its attack on Iraq, which was an attempt to distract the world from the clumsy actions that frustrated the mission to capture the people who truly caused the events of 9/11.

I speak of the same Bush who fomented and revived the obsession with the Middle East and who managed, as few others have, to completely ignore the reality of his country's closest neighbors. Indifferent, disrespectful, and superficial, the Bush team for Latin America generated only antipathy, rage, and ill will. Allies were mysteriously marginalized as the United States instead chose to exert control over foreign governments through elites instead of institutions. The worst sign of the increasing distance wrought between the United States and the region came, of course, with the construction of a wall along the country's much-feared border with Mexico, which brought to mind the memory and the consequences of other walls, like the one that divided Berlin in two.

Contrary to what some might think, Latin America, not the Middle East, is the region that the United States ought to be concerned about in the decades to come. Today, the region is a vast factory of poverty and famine. Presently there are six hundred million people living in the region, half of whom are poor. Imagine the entire population of the United States living in the most extreme hardship. It is a desperate circumstance that knows only disappointment and disillusion: eighty-one million are indigent and nine million live on one dollar a day. Year after year, forgotten and filled with doubt, three hundred thousand children die of hunger. Latin America has, according to one estimate, some 671 indigenous groups, an overwhelmingly abandoned sector that represents eighty percent of the most extreme poverty, despite the fact that, in many cases, these indigenous people share their territory with transnational mining and oil companies.

III.

At my side as I write this essay is the volume my father gave me, the Kennedy biography. It has not survived the years so well: its letters are no longer quite so gold, the green cloth is fading, certain chapters suffer from far too much underlining. Here and there, slipped in between its pages, are a few articles my father wrote about justice and his love for America, a country that despite everything he never knew in person. One note from 1964 reads, "I have never visited the United States, and by now I know I never will, but I shall keep that wish alive." Ironically for him, he was never able to get a visa to visit the country he so admired, though in his later years he was a judge and an active advocate of democracy. To the very end he would send postcards to his "gringo" friend and received postcards from his friend in return. One of the postcard photos featured images of Canaima and Salto Angel, the tallest waterfall in the world, named after Jimmy Angel, the American pilot who discovered it in one of those magnificent flights of happenstance.

And today? I know how much has been made of the need for strengthened relations between the United States and its Latin American neighbors, and I dare to suggest that the connections between the two regions must first be made more dignified somehow. Vast sums of money are invested in promoting the Free Trade Agreement, yet somehow people seem to forget that culture is the bridge between nations. Any kind of integration without honesty is an ambush. My own fear—supported by fact—is that the United States has been hijacked by a political class with a military vocation that long ago surrendered unconditionally to corporate interests that destroy the environment and manipulate the politics of entire continents, having given in to the commercialization of freedom rather than the freedom of commerce. As a result, no matter where I go, from the Rio Grande down to Tierra del Fuego, the influence of the United States has become mere compromise and has lost all credibility.

By way of an anecdote, I will conclude with a summary of what has been on my mind as well as what has been happening in the world of late. In 2004, on a visit to Mexico, I spent several long hours walking around the Zócalo, fascinated by the mysteries of its architecture. After a while, I decided it was time for a cold beer and found a tiny, noisy bar. As loud shouts erupted from all the tables, the wind swept unceremoniously through the place, whipping past those of us standing by the ancient entrance door. The television displayed the choppy images of a massive crater in Baghdad, formed by a homemade explosive device that had killed two soldiers, twenty and twenty-two years old. At my side, an old man from Jalisco said in a low voice: "My son was a musician, but he died in Fallujah. In a horrible, stupid combat, and the worst part of all is that I think he gave his blood to a country that was not wise enough to value his talents." He then showed me the photograph of a smiling young man. "The American dream can be a nightmare," he added and then withdrew. I listened to him, nodding my head without much energy, surprised by the disillusionment he had confided in me, and ordered another beer, which I wouldn't drink. I then walked over to the darkest corner of the bar and sat down, to wait hours and hours, with the same doubts and the inevitable nostalgia of someone who knows he is an émigré of the lost paradise of his memory.

About the Contributors

CHRIS ABANI, born in Nigeria, is the author of several works of poetry and prose, including most recently the novel *The Virgin of Flames* (Penguin, 2007) and the novella *Song for Night* (Akashic, 2007). A professor of creative writing at the University of California, Riverside, he is the recipient of many awards, among them the PEN USA Freedom-to-Write Award and the PEN Hemingway Book Prize.

RICARDO ALARCÓN is the president of the National Assembly of the Republic of Cuba. During Batista's regime, he was the student leader in the 26 of July Movement, the rebel group led by Castro. He graduated from Havana University with a degree in philosophy and literature and was Cuba's ambassador to the United Nations in New York for almost fifteen years. He became Cuba's foreign minister before being elected to his current job as president of the Cuban parliament.

FERNANDO BÁEZ, director of Venezuela's National Library, is a world authority on the history of libraries. In 2003 he visited Iraq as a member of the UN committee investigating the destruction of the country's libraries and museums. A prize-winning essayist, he is the author of numerous books and contributes to publications in thirty-two countries. His most recent book, *A Universal History of the Destruction of Books* (Atlas & Co., 2008), has been published in twelve countries.

A Palestinian poet born in 1944 in Ramallah, **MOURID BARGHOUTI** has published twelve books of poetry, the last of which is *Midnight*. Barghouti was awarded the Palestine Award for Poetry (2000) and the Naguib Mahfouz Medal for Literature for his memoir *I Saw Ramallah* (Anchor, 2003, introduction by Edward Said), which was translated into twelve languages. He has participated in many international poetry festivals and lectured in several Arab and European universities. He now lives in Cairo with his wife, the Egyptian novelist Radwa Ashour, and their son Tamim: www.mouridbarghouti.net.

ABDELKADER BENALI was born in Ighazzazen, Morocco, and has lived in the Netherlands since 1979. He is the author of several novels—among them *Wedding by the Sea*, *The Long-Awaited*, *May the Sun Shine Tomorrow*, and *Maxime Feldman and I*—as well as the nonfiction *Reports from a Besieged City* (that city being Beirut during the recent war) and *The Marathon Runner*. Benali has also written for the theater and published the story collection *Reports from Maanzaad Town*. He is winner of the Geertjan Lubberhuizen Prize, the Libris Prize, and the Prix du Premier Roman Etranger.

CARMEN BOULLOSA, born and raised in Mexico City, is a novelist, poet, and dramatist. Her work has been translated into nine languages. She is the author of a dozen novels, among them *Leaving Tabasco* (Grove, 2001) and *They're Cows, We're Pigs* (Grove, 1997). Her most recent book is *El Violín y la Virgen* (Siruela, 2008). A Guggenheim Fellow, she has been awarded many prizes, among them the Xavier Villaurrutia, the Liberatur of Frankfurt, and the Anna Seghers. She lives in New York, where she is a Distinguished Lecturer at CUNY and hosts the CUNY-TV show *Nueva York*. www.carmenboullosa.net

Novelist, memoirist, children's book author, and speaker DA CHEN was born and raised in China. He is the author of *Color of the Mountain* (Random House, 2000), *China's Son* (Delacorte Books for Young Readers, 2001), and *Sounds of the River* (HarperCollins, 2003) among others. His most recent novel is *Brothers* (Three Rivers Press, 2007). His books have been awarded numerous prizes and used as textbooks in many universities. He lives in the Hudson Valley in New York with his wife and two children.

IMRAAN COOVADIA was born in Durban, South Africa. He was educated at Harvard College and Yale and teaches English at the University of Cape Town. He is the author of two novels, *The Wedding* (Picador, 2001) and *Green-Eyed Thieves* (Umuzi, 2006), as well as a number of shorter pieces—stories, essays, academic articles, and book reviews—and a forthcoming monograph, *Authority and Authorship in V. S. Naipaul*.

GYÖRGY DRAGOMÁN was born in the Transylvania region of Romania in 1973, where he grew up as a member of the Hungarian minority. He immigrated to Hungary in 1988. A Samuel Beckett scholar and former film critic, he has translated works by Beckett, James Joyce, Ian McEwan, and Irvine Welsh into Hungarian. Dragomán's second novel, *The White King*, was awarded Hungary's prestigious Sándor Márai Prize in 2006; it was twice excerpted in the *Paris Review* and was published in the United States in 2008 by Houghton Mifflin. It is due to be published in twenty-five languages worldwide. Dragomán lives in Budapest with his wife, the poet Anna Szabó, and their two sons.

TERRY EAGLETON is the John Edward Taylor Professor of English Literature at Manchester University, UK, and was previously the Thomas Warton Professor of English Literature at Oxford. He lives in Dublin. He has published fifty or so books of literary criticism and cultural and political theory and wrote the screenplay for Derek Jarman's film *Wittgenstein*. He has taught frequently in the United States and has also had several plays produced on the London and Irish stage.

VICTOR EROFEYEV is the author of several novels, including *Russian Beauty* (Penguin, 1994), *The Good Stalin*, and *The Last Judgment*, and a collection of short stories, *Life with an Idiot* (Viking Adult, 2003). Editor of *The Penguin Book of New Russian Writing* (Penguin Books, 1995), he regularly contributes to the *Times*

Literary Supplement, the *New Yorker*, the *New York Review of Books*, and the *International Herald Tribune*. He lives in Moscow.

ALBERTO FUGUET is a Chilean-born, American-raised Chilean who has lived in Santiago de Chile since he was twelve. He has been a film critic and police reporter. Among his books translated into English are *Shorts* (HarperCollins, 2005), *Bad Vibes* (Rayo, 2003), and *The Movies of My Life* (St. Martins, 1997). A former writer-in-residence at UCLA, he has written for *Time*, the *Washington Post* and the *New York Times Magazine*, among other English-language publications. He has directed the feature film *Se Arrienda* and several video clips.

ZARAH GHAHRAMANI was born in Tehran in 1981, two years after Ayatollah Khomeini returned to Iran to establish the Islamic Republic. In 2001, after having taken part in student demonstrations, she was arrested and charged with "inciting crimes against the people of the Islamic Republic of Iran." Her interrogation in Evin Prison was harsh. Eventually she immigrated to Australia, where she now lives. She is the author of *My Life as a Traitor* (Farrar, Straus and Giroux, 2008, also released in several other countries and languages).

UZMA ASLAM KHAN grew up in Karachi and until recently had been living in Lahore, Pakistan. She is the author of *The Story of Noble Rot* (Penguin India, 2001), *Trespassing* (HarperCollins, 2004, published in eigh-

teen countries), and most recently *The Geometry of God* (Rupa, 2008). She has taught English language and literature in the United States, Morocco, and Pakistan and has contributed to various publications and anthologies. She currently lives in the United States.
http://uzmaaslamkhan.blogspot.com

ANDREÏ MAKINE was born in Siberia. Granted political asylum in France, he moved to Paris at the age of thirty, resolved to become a writer. His early work was rejected by publishers who doubted a genuine Russian immigrant could write eloquently in French. His third published novel, *Le testament français* (*Dreams of My Russian Summers*, Simon & Schuster, 1997), was the first to win both of France's most prestigious book awards, the Prix Goncourt and the Prix Medicis. His latest novel, *L'Amour humain*, was published in France in 2006.
www.andreimakine.com

LEILAH NADIR is Iraqi-Canadian and grew up in England and Canada. She is the author of the memoir *The Orange Trees of Baghdad: In Search of My Lost Family*, published in Canada in 2007 and more recently in Italy and Australia. She writes fiction and nonfiction and has published work in *Brick* magazine and the *Globe and Mail* and has broadcast stories and commentaries on CBC radio.

GIANNI RIOTTA was born and raised in Sicily. He worked at the daily newspaper *Il Manifesto* and studied logic at the University of Palermo and journalism at Columbia University. He is a contributor to various publications, including the *New York Times*, *Washington Post*, *Le Monde*, *El Pais*, and the *Wall Street Journal*. After many years as a correspondent and columnist for the Italian daily *Corriere della Sera*, he is editor of Tg1, Italy's oldest public TV news program. His novels *Prince of the Clouds* and *The Lights of Alborada* have been translated in many countries, including the United States. He teaches at the University of Bologna and is a member of the advisory council at the Department of French and Italian, Princeton University.

TOM SEGEV was born in Jerusalem. Segev's weekly column is published in *Ha'aretz*, Israel's leading daily newspaper. Segev is the author of six books that have been translated into eight languages, including *The Seventh Million—the Israelis and the Holocaust* and *One Palestine, Complete—Jews and Arabs under the British Mandate*, a *New York Times* Editors' Choice Best Book for 2000. Segev's most recent book is *1967—Israel, the War and the Year That Transformed the Middle East*. Segev has been a Fellow of the Humanities Council and the Department of History, Princeton University, and Diller Visiting Professor at the Center for Middle Eastern Studies and the Graduate School of Journalism, U.C. Berkeley.

SUNNY SINGH was born in Varanasi, India, and studied in the United States (Brandeis), New Delhi (Jawaharlal Nehru University), and Spain (Universitat de Barcelona). She now lives in London, where she teaches creative writing. Her articles and stories have appeared in various publications around the world. She is the author of the novels *Nani's Book of Suicides* (HarperCollins: India; Cobre: Spain, 2000) and *With Krishna's Eyes* (Rupa, 2006, and recently published in Spain, France, and Italy) and has contributed to several anthologies and publications around the world.

Journalist and author **WERNER SONNE** served as a foreign correspondent reporting from Bonn, Washington, and Warsaw. He first worked at UPI in Bonn and then moved to the radio division of West German Radio. He continued as a correspondent for ADR, Germany's national television and radio network. His books include *Allah's Revenge* (Ullstein, 1999), *Quote Game* (Ullstein, 1999), *Once Upon a Time in Germany* (Ullstein, 2000), and *Fatal Honor* (Ullstein, 2002).

LUÍS FERNANDO VERÍSSIMO was born in Porto Alegre, Brazil. He lived for a time in Berkeley and Washington DC. He started his career as a journalist and is still a frequent columnist and short-story (what Brazilians call *crônica*) writer. A respected journalist, cartoonist, and humorist, Luís Fernando Veríssimo has published several novels and short story collections. His most recent novel is *Borges and the Eternal Orangutans* (New Directions, 2005). http://portalliteral.terra.com.br/verissimo.

Acknowledgments

Assembling this anthology was the work of many hands, not least its editor and coconceiver John Oakes, who called upon his decades in the publishing world to cast a net that pulled in many of these luminous essays: among his far-flung sources were the agents Isobel Dixon of the Blake Friedmann Agency and Laura Susjin; also Chesa Boudin, who put us in touch with Ricardo Alarcón, President of the Cuban National Asembly. I called upon some trusty sources of my own, most notably Roberto Feith, the distinguished publisher of Objetiva in Brazil. Lukas Volger, Alex Rothman, Lauren LeBlanc, and Nataša Lekić made it happen—as they make all things happen at Atlas & Co.